Sacred Mysteries among the Mayas and the Quiches - 11, 500 Years Ago

In Times Anterior to the Temple of Solomon.

AUGUSTUS LE PLONGEON
(Originally published in 1886)

Introduction by MARSHAL MASON

Presented by **ithink books**
ithinkbooks@gmail.com

TABLE OF CONTENTS

Preface

Introduction by Marshal Mason

Author Note

Sacred Mysteries among the Mayas and the Quiches

PLONGEON

Preface

The forests of Yucatan and Central America are today, for the majority of the people of the United States, even those who call themselves scientific and well informed, as much a *terra incognita*, as America was to the inhabitants of Europe before its discovery by Cristobal Colon in 1498, when for the first time he came in sight of the northern coast of South America, and navigated along it from the mouth of the river Orinoco to *Porto Cabello* in the *Golfo Triste*.

A few, having perused the books of J. L. Stephens, Norman, and other tourists who have hurriedly visited the ruins of the ancient cities that lie hidden in the depths of those forests, have a vague idea that there exist the remains of stone houses built some time or other before the discovery, aver authoritatively that "their builders were but little removed from the state of savagism, and that none of their handwork is worth the attention of the students of our age. Their civilization, they confidently say, was at best very crude. They were ignorant of the art of writing; and the scanty records of their history chronicled on deer-skins, in pictorial representations, are well nigh unintelligible. They had no sciences, no mental culture or intellectual development. They were in fact a race whose intelligence was for the most part of lower order. From what they did nothing is to be learned that has any direct bearing on the progress of civilization." In no wise can they be compared with the Egyptians or the Chaldees, much less with the Greeks or Romans; it is not, therefore, worth our while to spend time and money in researches among the ruins of their cities. It is to Greece, it is to Egypt, to Chaldea, that Americans must go in order to make new discoveries. In those countries must be established schools for study of Greek, or Egyptian, or Chaldean archæology: and American schools have been established at Athens and Alexandria, and expeditions sent to Syria, to the shores of the Euphrates.

But the European scientists, who for many years past have explored those old fields in order to obtain relics to fill the shelves of the museums of their capitals and turned up the soil of the Orient in search of archæological treasures, now look to the Western continent in quest of the origin of those ancient civilizations which they have been unable to find in the countries where they once flourished; and they look with that reverence which true learning begets, on those ancient American temples and palaces that are objects of contempt for some modern American scientists.

Thus we see established in Paris the "*Société des Américanistes*" whose sole object is the study of all things pertaining to ancient American civilization. That Society, composed of students, spares no efforts to obtain knowledge respecting the architecture, the sciences, the arts, the language, and the civilization of the people who inhabited, in remote ages, the various countries of this Western continent. A premium of 25,000 francs has been offered for the discovery of an alphabet or key to the inscriptions carved on the walls of the monuments in Yucatan and Central America. M. Désiré Charnay has been sent to obtain molds of the sculptures and other precious relics that lie hidden and lost in the recesses of the Central American forests. Casts have been made from such squeezes as he obtained. These casts adorn the Trocadero Museum at Paris, duplicates of the same having been presented to the Smithsonian Institute at Washington by Mr. Pierre Lorillard of New York. This gentleman is the only American who has ever contributed with his wealth and influence (he has spent 25,000 dollars) in expeditions for the recovery of facts and objects that may throw light on the ancient history of America.

Then again we have in Europe the international "Congrès des Américanistes" that convenes every four years in one of the capitals of Europe for the purpose of collecting all new data, obtained in the interval, concerning ancient American civilization.

In England, at Cambridge, there is in the University a large building especially dedicated to Central American archæology. There are to be seen, as I am informed by General Sir Henry Lefroy, the casts and photographs obtained by Mr. Maudslay, a wealthy gentleman who has devoted his time and wealth to the work of obtaining *fac-similes* in plaster and photographs of the ancient monuments of Honduras and Guatemala.

But what have we in New York, in the United States, in fact, to offer to students of American archæology?

True, Mr. George Peabody, among his many benefactions, left a sum of money for the foundation of a museum to be specially dedicated to the collection of objects pertaining to American archæology. Such museum exists at the University of Cambridge, Massachusetts. It bears his name. Does it contain anything that may throw light on the history of the ancient inhabitants of this Western Continent? I once wrote to an influential gentlemen connected with the University asking him to propose to the trustees the purchase of a copy of my collections of casts and mural paintings. His answer dated July 23, 1885, was: "I will send your letter to one of the trustees, enjoining him to accept its offer, but I fear they will treat that proposal as they have so many others and say *no*! The collection of tracings they ought to secure. The time has come when such things should be got at any cost. We shall soon be as they are in India, hunting everywhere for things which were easily to be had a few years ago."

My correspondent has visited the ruined cities of Yucatan; he knows the value of my collections.

I have done all in my power to call the attention of American scientists, of the men of leisure and money, to the fact that in New York perfect fac-similes of the palaces and temples of the Mayas could be erected in Central Park, both as ornament to the place, and object of study for the lovers of American archæology who may not have the means, nor the time, nor the desire, to run the risk of submitting to the privations and hardships that those who wish to visit the ruined cities, must inevitably encounter.

But alas! all in vain.

Three years ago I had casts made from some of the stereotyped moulds made by me of the sculptures at Uxmal and offered them for exhibition in the Metropolitan Museum of Art in Central Park. They have been placed in the cellar, out of the way, "for want of space against the wall." The public has never seen them. I once remonstrated with one of the trustees, and proposed to sell to the museum a copy of the collection of fresco paintings from Chichen Itza, last remnants of ancient American art. The answer of the gentleman was "No! those things are not appreciated, they are looked upon as of no value." Nevertheless, some of the illustrations in this book are photographs of the same despised casts and mural paintings.

During the last lecturing season I offered to several literary, scientific and historical societies, to give lectures illustrated with views made by us of the monuments, and enlarged with the stereopticon. In every instance I received the same answer. "Our people are not interested in such a subject." What! Americans not interested in American antiquities! in ancient American history! in ancient American civilization!

Desiring to make the subject known before the lecture season was over, *en desespoir de cause*, I asked Dr. John Stoughton Newbury, of the School of Mines at Columbia College, if he could give me a chance to present the subject before the members of the New York Academy of Science. I had no hope of a favorable answer; but to my great surprise Professor Newbury received my offer enthusiastically. Mrs. Le Plongeon lectured on the monuments of Yucatan on the 2nd of March last, at Columbia College. Let the ladies and gentlemen who were present say if the facts and views presented to them were of sufficient interest to command their attention. A lady, Mrs. Francis B. Arnold, residing at 21 West 12th Street, New York, was so pleased that she asked Mrs. Le Plongeon to lecture at her own house to a select party of friends. Let again the ladies and gentlemen who were present at Mrs. Arnold's house, say if there is nothing worth seeing and studying in the remains of ancient American civilization.

Let Mrs. Arnold and Dr. Newbury accept our heartfelt-thanks for affording us an opportunity of presenting ancient America to a few appreciative minds, if no more.

Mrs. Le Plongeon and I have written two works on Yucatan. One is: "Monuments of Mayax, and their historical teachings." The other:

"Yucatan, its ancient palaces and modern cities; life and customs of the Aborigines." We have offered them to several publishing houses, but the same answer has been given by all. "There is no money in the publication of such books; American readers do not care for this subject."

Notwithstanding such rebuffs, I made up my mind to present to American readers some of the historical facts that have been brought to light by deciphering the bas-reliefs and mural inscriptions, by means of the ancient hieratic Maya alphabet discovered by me. I offer them in this small volume that I take pleasure in dedicating to Mr. Pierre Lorillard, as the most worthy of it among the Americans, for his generous help to students of American archæology.

If the perusal of this book fails to awaken in this country an interest in ancient American civilization and history, then I will follow the advice said to have been given by Jesus of Nazareth to his disciples when sending them on their mission of spreading the gospel among the nations: "And whomsoever shall not receive you, nor hear you, when ye depart thence, shake off the dust under your feet...." St. Mark, chap. vi., verse 11—for I shall consider it useless to spend more time, labor, and money on the subject in the United States, remembering the fate of Professor Morse, when he asked Congress for permission to introduce his electric telegraph in this country.

Introduction by Marshal Mason

Sacred Mysteries among the Mayas and the Quiches, by Augustus Le Plongeon, presents the ancient esoteric mysteries as rooted in South America, "Lands of the West", and not India, Chaldea, or Egypt as most scholars speculate. Augustus Le Plongeon pinpoints the Yucatan region as the origins and the Mayan people as the originators.

Augustus Le Plongeon, an expert of the Mayan language, arrives at this conclusion after spending twelve years researching the ancient temples and palaces of the Mayax, deciphering numerous inscriptions and symbols, and studying the sacred books of the Quiche People.

The author further explores the experiences of a person during the different stages of Initiation, and the reason numbers such as 3, 5, and 7 are considered sacred. The information Augustus Le Plongeon provides is valuable to every person interested in the ancient mysteries and the art of Initiation. But please be aware, Initiation is dangerous and not a path for the weak, the ill-informed, and the undisciplined.

The goal of Augustus Le Plongeon, was not only to discover the origins of the ancient esoteric mysteries, but also the roots of Free Masonry. The author suggests that the bricks that built the foundation of Free Masonry are the ancient mysteries. Here, the author shares several similarities between the two. Yet, is it possible that the different esoteric schools such as those of the Egyptians, Indians, Chaldeans, and Mayans did not originate from one people or one continent, but from The Spirit, and for this reason, although the languages might be different, the mysteries are the same across the planet. Is it possible that The Spirit guided the Architects of Free Masonic thought as well?

- Marshal Mason

PLONGEON

Author Note

In this small book (which two of the most prominent firms in New York have positively refused to publish believing it to be a bad speculation), I present only such facts as can be proved by the works of well-known writers ancient and modern, and by the inscriptions carved on stone by the Maya learned men and historians. It is for you, Reader, to judge if they are worthy of your consideration.

PLONGEON

Sacred Mysteries among the Mayas and the Quiches

There are authors who attribute the origin of modern Free Masonry to the followers of Pythagoras, because some of the speculations of that Philosopher concerning the meaning of the numbers are to be found in the esoteric doctrines taught in the masonic lodges. Others, on account of the Christian symbols that have been incorporated in the decoration of things pertaining to Masonry, following the Swedish system, say that the Essenes and first Christians founded it. Others, again, make it originate in the building of Solomon's temple, many Jewish names, emblems and legends, taken from the Bible, having found their way into the rites of initiation to several degrees. Others, still, make it go back to Adam. Ask them why—they do not know. While not a few, and I among them, earnestly believe that Masonry existed before Adam was created. I believe it, because I am convinced that this pretended ancestor of man is a myth—and has never existed. Thomas Payne and those of his school say that the Druids were the fathers of the craft; they being worshipers of the sun, moon and stars: and these jewels of the firmament being represented on the ceilings of the M☐ lodges. Dance of Villoison speaks of Herculaneum as its birth place, because of the many similarities that existed between the collegia of the Romans and the lodges of the operative Masons of the middle ages. Michael Andrew Ramsay, a Scotch gentleman, in a discourse delivered in Paris in 1740, suggested the possibility of the fraternity having its origin, in the time of the crusades, among the Knight Templars, and he explains it in this way:—

The Pope, Clement V., and Phillippe-le-bel, King of France, fearing the power of the Templars and coveting their immense wealth, resolved to destroy the Order. When, in 1308, Jacques de Molay, then Grand Master of the Order, was preparing an expedition to avenge the wrongs and disasters suffered by the Christians in the East, the Pope, who was the only power to which, in the spiritual, the Templars owed allegiance, enticed him to France.

On his arrival he was received with every mark of friendship: but, soon after, the King caused him to be arrested together with some of the other dignitaries, accusing them of the most heinous crimes, imputing to them the secret rites of their initiation. By order of the Archbishop of Sens and his provincial council, Jacques de Molay, Guy of Auvergne and several other officers of the Order were burned alive on March 18, 1314.

The Pope, by a bull dated on the 2d of April, and published on the 2d of May, 1312, that he issued on his own responsibility, the Council of Vienne, in Dauphiné, being adverse to hasty measures, declared the Order abolished throughout the world. The execution of the Grand Master and his companions gave the *coup de grace* to the Order. Some of the Knights who had escaped to Portugal continued the Order. They assumed the title of Knights of Christ, which it bears to this day; but it never recovered its former prestige and power.

Jacques de Molay, before dying had appointed Johan Marcus Larmenio as his successor to the office of Grand Master. The Knights who, fleeing from the persecution, had taken refuge in Scotland at the Court of King Robert Bruce, refused to recognize his authority; and pretending to reëstablish the Order of the Temple, under the allegory and title of Architects, protected by the King, laid the foundation of the Order of Free and Accepted Masons of the Scottish Rite in 1314.

This new society soon forgot the meaning of the execratory oath that the members were obliged to take at their initiation; the death of Clement V., of Phillippe-le-bel, of the accusers and enemies of Jacques de Molay and the other Knights who had been executed, having removed the object of their vengeance. Still they continued to decorate their lodges with tokens commemorative of the death of the Grand Master, to impose on all new members the obligation of avenging it, which they signified by striking with an unsheathed dagger at unseen beings, his supposed murderers, although all their efforts were now directed to the restoration of the honor of their association. This allegory is well-known to the Knights of Kadosh. A century had scarcely elapsed when this idea also was abandoned, the founders and their disciples having passed away. Their successors saw only allegories in the symbols of the Order, and the extensive use of words and texts from the Bible was then introduced. Of their work but little is positively known until the reign of Charles I. of England, when their mysterious initiations began to attract attention.

The enemies of Cromwell and of the Republic, having in view the reëstablishment of the monarchy, created the degree of Grand Master to prepare the minds of the Masons for that event. King William III. was initiated. Masonry, says Preston, was very much neglected as early as the reign of James II., and even after this period it made but slow progress until 1714, when King George I. ascended the throne.

Three years later, in February, 1717, the first Grand Lodge was established in London. A committee from the four lodges then existing in that city met at the tavern of the "Apple Tree" and nominated Anthony Sayer, who was elected Grand Master on the 24th of the following June, day of St. John the Baptist, that for this reason was selected as patron of the Order.

This origin of the craft is credited by many of the best authorities on the subject. They found their opinion on the fact that many of the ceremonies practiced by the *Architects* are still observed among the Masons; and that the Grand Lodge preserved, with the spirit of the ancient brotherhood, its fundamental laws. There are others, however, who likewise claim to be well informed, that pretend it did not originate in any order of chivalry, but in the building fraternities of the Middle Ages.

Be the origin what it may, the fact is that after the establishment of the Grand Lodge at "Apple Tree Tavern," Masonry spread over Europe at a rapid rate, notwithstanding the bitter opposition of the Church of Rome that fulminated against it its most terrible anathemas as early as 1738 at the instigation of the Inquisition. Pope Clement XII., on the 28th of April of that year, caused a prohibitory bull to be issued against Free Masonry, entitled *In Eminenti*, in which he excommunicated all Masons; and the

Cardinal Vicar of Rome, by edict in the name of the High Priest of the God of Peace and Mercy, decreed the penalty of death against them in 1739; and on May 18, 1751, Pope Benoit XIV. renewed the bull of Clement XII. by another beginning with these words: *Providas Romanorum Pontificum.*

The Order was introduced in France in 1725, and on the 14th of September, 1732, all Masonic Associations were prohibited by a decree of the Chamber of Police of the Chatelet of Paris.

In 1727, Lord Coleraine founded a lodge in Gibraltar, and in the succeeding year in Madrid, the capital of Spain, the strong-hold of the Inquisition.

But in 1740, in consequence of the bull of Clement XII., King Philip V., of Spain, promulgated an ordinance against the Masons in his kingdom, many of whom were arrested and sent to the galleys. The Inquisitors took advantage of the opportunity to persecute the members of a lodge they discovered in Madrid. They caused them to be loaded with chains, to be obliged to row in the galleys without other retribution than scanty rations of victuals of the poorest quality, but an abundant supply of bastinade. Fernando VI. renewed the ordinance on July 2, 1751, making Masonry high treason.

The brotherhood made its appearance in Ireland in 1730. It is not positively known if it existed in the country before that time.

In 1732 it crossed the Atlantic and was imported in America. In that year a lodge was held in "Tun tavern" in Philadelphia, the B☐ having previously met in Boston, which may be regarded as the birthplace of American Free Masonry. Henry Price was the first provincial Grand Master appointed by the Grand Lodge of England on April 30th, 1733.

The same year witnessed its establishment in various cities of Italy. In 1735, the Grand Duke Francis of Lorraine was initiated. He protected the Masons, and the craft flourished in Italy until 1737, when Juan Gaston of

Medicis, Grand Duke of Tuscany, issued a decree of prohibition against it. Soon after his death, which occurred the same year, the lodges which had been closed were reopened. It was not long, however, before they were denounced to the Pope Clement XII., who issued his bull of 28th of April 1738, and sent an inquisitor to Florence who caused various members of the society to be cast into dungeons. They were set at liberty as soon as Francis of Lorraine became Grand Duke of Tuscany. He not only protected the Masons, but founded lodges in Florence and other places in his estates.

In 1735 a lodge was established in Lisbon the capital of Portugal. It will be remembered that some of the Knight Templars, under the title of "Knights of Christ," had kept alive the ancient order in that country in defiance of the Pope's thunderbolts.

Among the Masons initiated in England were a great many Germans as early as 1730. These seem to have met occasionally in traveling in Germany, or to have corresponded with each other; but no lodge is known to have existed previous to the year 1737, when one without name was established in Hamburg, although Grand Master Lord Strathmore had authorized in 1733, eleven gentlemen and Brothers to open one.

In 1740, B. Puttman, of the Hamburg lodge, received a patent of Provincial Grand Master from England, and the lodge assumed the title of Absalom.

King Frederick II., denominated the Great, whilst still Crown Prince, had been initiated; and from the time of his initiation took great interest in the welfare of the brotherhood. Crowned King of Prussia, he continued to give it his support, assuming the title of "*Great master universal, and Conservator of the most ancient and most respectable association of ancient free masons or architects of Scotland*." Masonry enjoyed under his reign such consideration, that many German princes, following his example, were initiated; and so many of the nobility joined the society, that to belong to it came to be regarded as a mark of nobility and high breeding.

Notwithstanding his multifarious State duties, and the many wars that took place during his reign, which demanded his constant attention, he found time to frame a constitution to cement together again the Order, that at one time, owing to external persecutions on the one hand, to internal dissensions, suscitated by the incorporation to it of the Rosicrucians and still more that of the *Illuminati* on the other, seemed on the eve of falling asunder. That constitution, signed by him in his palace at Berlin, on the 1st of May, 1786, saved Free Masonry from annihilation in Germany, for many regarding it with suspicion, attacked and persecuted it: the Catholics because it came from Protestant England; the Protestant clergy looked upon it as hostile to Christianity, because of the teachings and symbols altogether Catholic of the 18th degree, those of Rosa Cruz, whose motto "we have the happiness of being in the pacific unity of the sacred numbers," and "in the name of the holy and indivisible Trinity," bespeaks its Jesuit origin. The people believed in the accusation of witchcraft and sorcery, made against it by its enemies, because of the vail of secrecy thrown over their meetings.

Authors have endeavored to show that modern free-masonry is not derived from the mysteries of the ancients. J. G. Findel, an advocate of this opinion, says: "Seeing that the ancient symbolical marks and ceremonials in the lodges bear a very striking resemblance to those of the mysteries of the ancients some have allowed themselves to be deceived, and led others astray imagining they can trace back the history of the craft into the cloudy mists of antiquity. Instead of endeavoring to ascertain how and when these ceremonies were introduced into our present system, they have taken it for granted that they were derived from the religious mysteries of the ancients."

Now, if we merely consider the tokens of recognition, the pass words and secret words, the decorations of the lodges, according to the degrees into which modern Masonry is divided, tokens, words and decorations nearly all taken from the Bible and symbolical of events, real or imaginary, some of which are said to have taken place in comparatively modern times, after the decline and final discontinuance of the ancient mysteries in consequence of the spread of Christianity; others having occurred in the early days of the Christian era; others at the time of the building of Solomon's Temple, all of

Sacred Mysteries among the Mayas and the Quiches

which had certainly nothing to do with the religious mysteries of Egypt, Chaldea, Greece, Etruria, etc., that were instituted ages before the pretended occurrence of those events, then we may positively affirm that it is not derived from these. But if, on the other hand, we observe, and it is difficult to overlook it, that these symbols are precisely the same that we find in the temples of Egypt, Chaldea, India, and Central America, whatever may have been the esoteric meaning given to them by the initiated of those countries, we are bound to admit that a link exists between the ancient mysteries and Free Masonry. It is for us to try to discover when that link was riveted and by whom.

If the theory of Chevalier Ramsay be true, that is, if modern Masonry had its beginning in the Society of Architects founded in Scotland under the protection of King Robert Bruce, and the title of "Ancient and Accepted Masons of the Scottish rite," seems to favor that opinion, then we may trace its origin to the order of Knight Templars; and through them to the ancient mysteries practiced in the East from times immemorial. It is well known that one of the charges made against Jacques de Molay and his associates by their accusers was that they used secret rites in their initiations. Their four oaths were well known; but not their rites of initiation. What were they?

We are told that the aim of the Society of Architects was to perpetuate the ancient Order of the Temple. It is therefore to be presumed that they continued to observe the rites and ceremonies practiced in the chapters of the Templars, to use them at the initiations of members into the new Society, to whom they communicated the intimate meaning of their symbols. Were these rites analogous to those observed in the initiations to the symbolical degrees? These degrees were, it must be remembered, the only ones originally recognized by the brotherhood; as there are but three in the Society of Jesus; the Neophites—the Coadjutors—and the Profess; as there were anciently among the priests of the temples of Egypt, who indeed considered it a great honor to be judged worthy of admission to the third degree; that is, to participation in the greater mysteries. Was their explanation of the symbols similar to that taught in M☐ lodges? The

Templars were accused, as Masons are to day, by the Romish Church, since it has lost its hold and influence on the association, of the crime of heresy, and many Masons have suffered death by being burnt alive as heretics.

From whom did the Templars receive those symbols, and their esoteric meaning, in which we plainly trace the doctrine of Pythagoras? No doubt from the Christians who, like the Emperor Julian, the Bishop Synnesius, Clement of Alexandria and many other pagan philosophers, who had been initiated to the mysteries by the priests of Egypt, before being converted to Christianity. In that case the connection of modern Masonry with the ancient religious mysteries of Egypt, consequently with those of Greece and Samothracia is easily traced; and the resemblance of the symbolical marks and ceremonials of M☐ lodges with those of the mysteries naturally accounted for. Thus it is that many masonic authors may have been led to trace the origin of the craft to followers of Pythagoras; and others to the Essenes and first Christians.

Krause, in his work, has endeavored to prove that Masonry originated in the associations of operative masons that in the Middle Ages travelled through Europe, and by whom the cathedrals, monasteries, and castles were built; whose fundamental laws, traditions, customs and tools are now used in the lodges in a figurative sense.

These associations may have sprung from the building corporations of the Romans: if so, we have a connecting link between the lodges of the Middle Ages and the mysteries of the ancients. The initiates of the architectural collegia of the Romans did not call themselves Brothers; this is a title that came into use only when the Christian Masonic fraternities adopted it. They styled themselves *Collega* or *Incorporatus*.

They worked in buildings apart or in secluded rooms; and the constitution of M☐ lodges, so far as the officers, their titles and duties, and the symbols are concerned, is so similar to theirs that one might be inclined to believe that the early Masons imitated the Roman collegia.

This theory is not without semblance of plausibility. Rome, during several centuries, held sway over Gaul and Britain. Roman colonists settled in various parts of those countries. With their language and customs they imported many of their institutions and associations. That of the builders or collegia, as is manifest from the remains still existing of the magnificent roads and edifices of various kinds constructed by them. The Collegæ held their lodges wherever they established themselves; no doubt initiated new members. In the course of time, when those countries freed themselves from the yoke of Rome, these societies of builders became the associations of the itinerant operative masons which inherited the symbols, tokens and pass words of the Collegæ. These, in all probability, had received them, either from the Chaldean magicians, who flocked to Rome at the beginning of the Christian era, when the progress of philosophical incredulity had shaken the confidence in legal divination; or from some of the priests of inferior order, all initiated to part of the lesser mysteries, that, when the sacerdotal class having lost in majesty, power and wealth, in order to preserve whole its numerous hierarchy, repaired to the Capital of the world to escape misery by levying contributions on the credulity and superstition of the people.

The Christian Church, on the one hand, the Roman emperors on the other, fearing the influence of those magicians and priests, persecuted them even to death. These learned and wise men formed secret societies to preserve and transmit their knowledge. These societies lasted during the Middle Ages—the Rosicrucians, the Theurgists, among them. Leibnitz, one of the greatest men of science that ever lived, who died in Hanover, in 1716, at the age of seventy years, became a member of one of these societies; and there received an instruction he had vainly sought elsewhere.

Were their mysterious meetings remnants of the ancient learned initiations? Everything tends to make us suspect it. The trials and examinations to which those who applied for initiation were obliged to submit; the nature of the secrets they possessed; the manner in which they were preserved. In these again may be found an explanation of why so many of the Pythagorean doctrines made their way into Masonry.

Of the ceremonies performed at the initiation into the mysteries of Egypt we know but little at present, for the initiated were very careful to conceal these sacred rites. Herodotus tells that if any person divulged any part of them, he was thought to have called down Divine judgment upon his head, and it was accounted unsafe to abide in the same house with him. He was even apprehended as a public offender and put to death.

Still, on reading the visions in the book of Henoch, and comparing them with what we know of the trials to which were subjected the applicants for initiation into the greater mysteries of Eleusis and Egypt, and those of Xibalba, one can scarcely refrain from believing that, under the title of Visions, the author relates his experience at the initiation, and what he learned in the mysteries before being converted to Christianity. That book is believed to have been written at the beginning of the Christian era, when, under the yoke of the Roman emperors, the customs and religion of the Egyptians fell into decadency; and the Christian bishops of Alexandria, such as George, Theophilus, Cyril, the murderer of the beautiful, learned and noble Hypathia, daughter of the mathematician Theon, persecuted the worshipers of Isis and Osiris, and converted their temples into Christian churches, after defacing and whitewashing the ancient sculptures that covered their walls, on which they painted rough images of saints. It may be that its author, although having embraced Christianity, still retained in his heart of hearts a strong love for the ancient institutions that were fast disappearing in the midst of the political and religious dissensions that were raging at the time. Fearing lest the learning of the priests of old and the knowledge he had acquired by his initiation into the mysteries should become lost, the dread of death being removed by the new order of things, he put, for greater safety, in the mouth of Henoch, as instructing his son, what he had seen and learned in the secrecy of the temples.

Let us hope that further discoveries in the ruins of the temples, or in the tombs, may put into our possession some papyrus whose contents will throw light on the subject, and reveal these secrets. The masonic objects found under the base of the obelisk, known as Cleopatra's needle, now in Central Park, New York, show that many of the symbols pertaining to the rites of modern Free Masonry, were used in Egypt by building organizations and architects at least 1900 years ago. And although I do not agree with all the conclusions of Dr. Fanton, notwithstanding they are approved by some of the high masons at Cairo and Alexandria, I am ready to recognize many of the emblems, and admit that they belonged to the mysteries, if their meaning anciently was not quite the same as we give them today.

The reluctance of the Egyptians to admit strangers to the holy secret of their mysteries was for a very long time insuperable. However, they seem to have relaxed at rare intervals, in favor of personages noted for their wisdom and knowledge. So they admitted the great philosopher Thales, who went to Egypt to learn geometry and astronomy, about 587 years before the Christian era. Eumolpus, king of Eleusis, who, on returning to his country, instituted the mysteries of that name in honor of the goddess Ceres, that presided over the crops and other fruits of the earth. Orpheus, the celebrated Greek poet, obtained likewise the honor of the initiation, and established the Orphic ceremonies, which, according to Herodotus, were observed alike by the Egyptians and the Pythagoreans. It must be remembered that Pythagoras, after being submitted to extremely severe ordeals, to cause him to desist from his desire of being initiated, was, on account of his firmness, granted the privilege of initiation. Many of the rites and ceremonies were therefore brought from Egypt to Greece. Speaking of the Thesmophoria festivals in honor of Ceres, next in importance to the mysteries of Eleusis, Herodotus says: "These rites were brought from Egypt into Greece by the daughters of Danaus, who taught them to the Pelagic women; but in the course of time they fell into disuse, except among the Arcadians who continued to preserve them. The Pelasgians had also initiated the inhabitants of Samothracia. They in turn taught the Athenians the mysteries of the 'Cabiri.'"

From that it results that if we desire to obtain an insight of the Egyptian mysteries, we must see what happened at the initiation into those of Greece.

No one could be admitted to the greater unless they had been purified at the lesser, and one year at least had elapsed since they had become *mystai* or initiated.

The initiation to the greater mysteries when the *Mystai* took the degree of *Ephoroi*, that is Inspector, by being instructed in the secret rites, except a few reserved for the priests alone, was as follows:

The candidate, being crowned with myrtle, which was used instead of the acacia, was admitted by night into an immense building called the *Mystikos Sêkos*, that is the "mystical enclosure." At their entrance they purified themselves by washing their hands in holy water, being at the same time admonished to present themselves with minds pure and undefiled, without which external cleanliness of the body would by no means be accepted. After this the holy mysteries were read to them from a book called *Petrôma*, because the book consisted of two stones fitly cemented together. I have discovered such stones, last year, in the mausoleum of high pontiff *Cay*, in the city of Chichen-Itza, in Yucatan. The priest who conducted the ceremonies was called *hierophantês*. He proposed certain questions, to which answers were returned in a set form. Then, strange and amazing objects presented themselves. Sometimes the place they were in seemed to shake, as if an earthquake was occurring, or whirl round and round as if carried away in a tornado. Sometimes it appeared bathed in bright and resplendent light, and flames seemed to issue from the walls, threatening to consume the temple; and all of a sudden they were extinguished by invisible hands, and the most profound obscurity succeeded to the dazzling radiance. Flashes of lightning, at intervals, broke forth with extreme brilliancy, only to make the darkness more dark, when peal after peal of thunder caused the building to shake to its very foundations. These were succeeded by loud cries for help and laments of persons in great agony; soon to be replaced by the most frightful noises and bellowings, and terrible apparitions. The nerves of the applicants were tried to the utmost, and required to be strung by the most indomitable will and moral as well as physical courage, to enable them to withstand to the last such awful trials.

All the faint hearted were invariably rejected and refused admission to the next degree, the *Epopteia*, or Inspection. Powerful narcotic drugs were administered to the timorous, that plunged them into a deathlike sleep, from which they emerged with but confused recollections, if not entire forgetfulness, of the terrible scenes they had witnessed, and which they believed to be produced by some frightful dream or dreadful nightmare.

I will now quote from the book of Henoch. Chap. xiv. ver. 12.—"I saw a spacious habitation built with stones of crystal. The roof had the appearance of agitating stars and flashes of lightning. Flames burnt around its walls, its portals blazed with fire. This dwelling was hot as fire—cold as ice." Chap. xvii. ver. 1.—"They raised me up into a certain place where there was the appearance of burning fire, and when they pleased, they assumed the likeness of men,—(ver. 3)—and I beheld the receptacles of light and of thunder at the extremities of the place. There was a bow of fire and arrows in their quiver—a sword of fire and every species of lightning."

Chap. xxi. vers. 4.—"Then I passed to another terrific place—(ver. 5)—where I beheld the operation of a great fire blazing and glittering, in the midst of which there was a division—columns of fire struggled together to the end of the abyss and deep was their descent. (Ver 6.)—This was the place of suffering."

Those who resisted to the last the trials of the *Autopsia*, as the initiation was called, were then dismissed with these three words: *Kon-x Om Pan-x*, which, strange to say, have no meaning in the Greek language. Captain Wilford, in his Essay on Egypt, says they correspond to the words *Cansha Om Pansha*, which the Brahmins pronounce every day to announce to the devotees that the religious ceremonies are over. They have been translated, "retire, O retire, profane!" Corresponding to the *ite missa est* of the Catholic Church.

These words are not Sanscrit, but Maya. "*Con-ex Omon Panex*," go, stranger, scatter! are vocables, of the language of the ancient inhabitants of Yucatan, still spoken by their descendants, the aborigines of that country.

They were probably used by the priests of the temples, whose sumptuous and awe-inspiring ruins I have studied during fourteen years, to dismiss the members of their mystic societies, among which we find the same symbols that are seen even today in the temples of Egypt as in the M☐ lodges.

I will endeavor to show you that the ancient sacred mysteries, the origin of Free Masonry consequently, date back from a period far more remote than the most sanguine students of its history ever imagined. I will try to trace their origin, step by step, to this continent which we inhabit,—to America—from where Maya colonists transported their ancient religious rites and ceremonies, not only to the banks of the Nile, but to those of the Euphrates, and the shores of the Indian Ocean, not less than 11,500 years ago.

But let us return to the mysteries of Eleusis. In the trials to which the *Mystai* were subjected to try their fitness to become *Ephoroi,* Masons no doubt recognize several of the ceremonies that took place at their initiation into the craft. If Free Masonry had not its origin in the ancient Sacred Mysteries, how could these rites have found their way into it?

The Ephoroi were now prepared for the third degree, the *Epopteia*—the most sacred of all. In this the *Epoptai* or "Inspectors of themselves" were placed in presence of the gods, who were supposed to appear to the initiated. Proclus, a philosopher, disciple of the divine Plato, in his commentaries on the Republic of his master, says: "In all initiations and mysteries, the gods exhibit themselves under many forms, and appear in a variety of shapes. Sometimes their unfigured light is held forth to view. Sometimes this light appears under a human form, and sometimes it assumes a different shape." And again, in his commentaries on the first Alcibiades: "In the most holy of the mysteries, before the god appears, the impulsions of certain terrestrial demons become visible, alluring the initiated from undefiled good to matter." Then all the seductions that human mind can imagine to excite the passions were placed within the grasp of those who aspired to become Epoptai. They were invited to freely give way to voluptuousness, to the enjoyment of all kind of mundane pleasures, before they renounced them forever. Nothing that could possibly entice applicants to fall from their state of moral and physical purity was omitted; all that could be done to induce them to yield to temptation was resorted to. If in a moment of weakness they allowed their senses to obtain the mastery over their reason, woe to them! for before they could realize their position, before they had time to recall their scattered thoughts, the bright surroundings disappeared as by magic; they were plunged in the most dense obscurity; the ground gave way under their feet; and they were precipitated into a deep abyss, from which if they escaped with their life, they never did with their reason.

Theon of Smyrna, in his work Matematica, divides the mysteries into five parts.

1. The purification.

2. The reception of sacred rites.

3. The Epopteia, or reception.

4. End and design of the revelation, the building of the head and fixing of the crowns.

5. The friendship and interior communion with God, the last and most awful of all the mysteries.

It is supposed the prophet Ezekiel alludes to these initiations, when he speaks of the abominations committed by the idolatrous ancients of the house of Israel in the dark, every man in the chambers of its imagery.

Here again, I will quote from the book of Henoch: Chap. xxii.—"From thence I proceeded to another spot where I saw on the West a great and lofty mountain, a strong rock and four delightful places."

Chap. xiv. ver. 14.—"Then I went to another habitation more spacious than the former. Every entrance which was opened before me was erected in the midst of a vibrating flame. Ver. 18.—Its floor was on fire, above were lightning and agitated stars, whilst its roof exhibited a blazing fire. Ver. 21.—One of great glory sat upon the orb of the brilliant sun. Ver. 24.—A fire of great extent continued to rise up before him."

It is said that the ordeal through which the candidates were obliged to pass previous to admission into the Egyptian mysteries, were even more severe, and that Pythagoras, wise philosopher as he was, had a narrow escape from it.

The priests alone could arrive at a thorough understanding of the mysteries. So sacred were their secrets held that many of the members of the sacerdotal order, even, were not admitted to a participation of them; but those alone who proved themselves deserving of the honor; since Clement of Alexandria, tells us: "the Egyptians neither entrusted their mysteries to every one, nor degraded the secrets of divine matters by disclosing them to the profane, reserving them for the heir apparent to the throne, and for such of the priests as excelled in virtue and wisdom."

From all we can learn on the subject, the mysteries consisted of two kinds, the greater and the lesser, divided into many classes. The candidate for initiation had to be pure, his character without blemish. He was commanded to study such lessons as tended to purify the mind. Great was the honor of ascending to the greater mysteries and it was difficult to attain to it. An inscription of a high priest at Memphis, says Mr. Samuel Birch, states: "That he knew the arrangements of the Earth, and those of Heliopolis and Memphis; that he had penetrated the mysteries of every sanctuary; that nothing was concealed from him; that he adored God and glorified Him in all His works, and that he hid in his breast all that he had seen." Had he not kept his secrets so carefully concealed, no doubt he would have told us that at one of the initiations the figure of the god Osiris, in whose honor the mysteries were celebrated, and whose name the initiates did not dare pronounce, appeared to the candidate, as it did at Heliopolis to Pianchi, king of Ethiopia.

At a later period, when the ancient customs had become relaxed owing to the invasion of the country by foreigners and to the government passing from the hands of native rulers to those of Persian, of Greek or Roman governors, many, besides the priests, came to be admitted to the lesser mysteries. But all had to pass through the different grades and conform to the prescribed rules, as in the case of Thales, Eumolpus, Orpheus, Pythagoras, Plato, Herodotus and others.

I will not here describe at length the initiations to the mysteries in honor of the Sun God, Mithra, instituted by Zoroaster, but only state that Porphyrius, on the testimony of Eubulus, says that this philosopher and reformer having selected a cavern in a pleasant locality in some mountains near Persia, dedicated it to Mithra, the Sun, creator and father of all beings; that he divided it into geometrical figures intended to represent the climates and elements; in a word that he imitated in a small way the order and disposition of the universe by Mithra. After him, it became customary to consecrate caverns for the celebration of mysteries; as we see yet in Japan.

The candidates for initiation to the Mithra mysteries were submitted to the most awful trials—among which one was to try the docility and courage of the applicant. He was ordered by the priest to kill a man. According to Plutarch, in his life of Pompeius, these mysteries were brought to the Occident by Cilician pirates about sixty-eight years before the Christian era. They were well received by the Greco-Latin world, and the initiated were soon to be counted by thousands. In the time of the Emperor Adrian, the mysteries of Mithra had become so popular that Pallas, a Greek writer, composed a poem on the subject, that Porphyrius has preserved in a special treatise on the abstinence from the use of animal flesh.

The mysterious initiations vividly impressed the imagination, as at times and by way of expiation, human victims were offered and immolated. The ceremonies of the priests consisted, says Origenes, in imitating the motions of the celestial bodies, those of the planets, in fact of the heavens. The initiated took the names of the constellations and dressed themselves as animals. A theology purely astronomical was taught in these mysteries, in which they used the purification by water in honor of the goddess *Ardvi çoura anâhita*, "She of the celestial waters;" the confession of sins; and a sort of eucharist, or offering of bread, still observed by the Parsis or fire worshippers in India. It may be said that during the last years of the Roman Empire, the religion of Mithra had become the state religion. It is not, therefore, to be wondered at, if it extended to the Roman provinces of Gaul and Britain, and if some of its rites have found their way into Free Masonry, and are practised to the present day; thus again relating it with very ancient sacred mysteries, established by Zoroaster, the author of the Zend-Avesta at least 1,100 years before Christ, although Hermippus, the Greek translator of his work, places him 5,000 years before the taking of Troy.

If we go to Hindostan, there we will learn of a secret society of wise and learned men, whose object is the study of philosophy in all its branches, but particularly the spiritual development of man. The leading fraternity is established in Thibet; and the high pontiff and other dignitaries of the Lama religion belong to it. They are known throughout India by the name of *Mahatmas* or Brothers. To obtain this title it is necessary to suffer a long and weary probation, and pass through ordeals of terrible severity. Many of the *Chelas*, as the aspirants are called, have spent twenty, even thirty years of blameless and arduous devotion to their task, and still they are in the earlier degrees, looking forward to the happy day when they may be judged worthy to have the title of Brother conferred upon them.

These *Mahatmas* are the successors of those secret societies of learned Brahmins, so celebrated for their wisdom, from very remote ages, in India; and of whose colleges or lodges, always built on the summit of high mounds, either natural or artificial, Alexander, the Great, when he achieved the conquest of that country, was never able to take possession. Philostratus informs us, that their mode of defense consisted in surrounding themselves with clouds, by means of which they could at will render themselves visible or not, and hurling from their midst tempests and thunder on their enemies.

Evidently in those early times, they had discovered gunpowder, or some other explosives of like nature, and made use of them to explode mines, and destroy their assailants. These same Brahmins claimed to have been the teachers of the Egyptians, who, according to that, would have received their civilization and scientific knowledge from them, as also did the Chaldeans. It is well known that the Magi were strangers who came to Babylon, possessors, says the prophet Daniel, not only of a special learning, but of a peculiar tongue. They formed a powerful society, into which at the beginning none but those of their own people were admitted, as their science was both exclusive and hereditary. A certain religious character was attached to the whole body; every priest must be a Chaldean, but every Chaldean was not a priest. They passed their whole lives in meditating questions of philosophy. Astronomy was their favorite study; but they acquired great reputation for their astrology. They were versed in the arts of prophesying, of explaining dreams and prodigies, and the omens furnished by the entrails of victims offered in sacrifice. The parents taught the children. At their head was a high pontiff with the title of *Rab-mag*, Venerable, or according to its meaning in the Maya language, *Lab-mac, "the old man."* At Babylon they were the ruling order, the advisers of the King. Nothing is known today of their rites of initiation; but they must have been very similar to those of the Egyptians, since the civilization of Chaldea and that of Egypt were twin sisters; offspring from the same parents.

I have endeavored in a cursory manner to show that the ancient sacred mysteries were established for the same purpose in every civilized nation of antiquity, that is for the cultivation of science; the acquirement of knowledge; the bettering of man's moral and physical nature; the development of his intellectual and mental faculties; the understanding and study of the laws that govern the material and spiritual world, thus bringing him into closer contact with Deity. They kept their learning and discoveries a profound secret, surrounding them with mysterious allegories, and enigmatical symbols, for, as says Strabo: "to surround the things that are holy with a mysterious obscurity is to make Divinity venerable, is to imitate its nature that escapes man's senses," or, as Gregory of Nazianze, wrote to

Jerome: "the less ignorant men understand the more they admire," and as the priests of today, in fact of all times, of all religions, they wished to be regarded by the masses as dispensers of the god's favors, as mediators between the Deity and man.

This similarity of the rites practiced in the initiations, the identity of symbols, proves that these rites and symbols had been communicated from one to another, just as in modern Free Masonry the initiations are the same in the lodges, the world over, having been carried to the most distant lands, by travelers, colonists or missionaries, from the fountain head, the Grand Lodge of England.

But with respect to the ancient Sacred Mysteries, the query arises as to where they originated. We know that from Egypt and Chaldea they were brought to Greece and Rome. From whom did the Egyptians and Chaldeans receive them? The Brahmins asserted that the Magi and the Hierophants were their disciples.

Admitting this assertion to be true, may we not ask, from whom did the Brahmins learn them? No doubt, if we question them on the subject, they will answer that they are the originators of these mystic rites, and secret societies of learned men; and with difficulty we could gainsay their assertion, were it not that Plutarch and other Greek writers, who have described the Eleusinian mysteries, have taken care to preserve the words used at the closing of the ceremonies by the officiating priest; and also made known to us the name and shape they gave to their place of meeting.

It is well known that the Brahmins, in many of their religious ceremonies, make use of words that are not Sanscrit, but are said to belong to a very ancient form of speech—now dead—the *Akkadian*, spoken by the inhabitants of the countries situated along the banks of the Euphrates, near its mouth. Strange as it may appear, this language presents many affinities with the Maya, which is still the vernacular of the aborigines of Yucatan and other countries south of the Peninsula. The fact is that the words *con-x—om—pan-x*, mean nothing in Greek, but, as we have said, are pure Maya vocables, that have the same meaning as that given to *can-sha—om—Pansha* by Captain Wilford.

That is not all. We are also told that the place or temple where the initiated assembled to perform their ceremonies, had the form of a rectangle, and that it represented the "Universe." Modern Masons have wrongly translated that idea by the Sanscrit word *loga*, from which the word *lodge* has been derived, and the form of M☐ lodges adopted.

The shape of the temples was that of the Egyptian letter *M* called "*ma*", a word that also means place, country and, by extension, the Universe. The Egyptians adopted it, therefore, not because they believed, as Dr. Fanton suggests, that the earth was square or *oblong*, for they knew full well it was spherical, but because the sign of the word *ma'*, conveyed to their mind the idea of the Earth, as the word *earth* represents it to ours. But *ma* is also the radical of Mayax; and likewise, in the Maya language, it means the country, the Earth. The Mayas selected the oblong square to represent it, because it is the geometrical figure that is nearest in shape to the contours of the Yucatecan peninsula.

So we have found a bridge to cross the vast expanse of water that lies between the Eastern and Western Continents—a clue that may lead us to the birth-place of the ancient sacred mysteries in those "Lands of the West," that "Land of *Kui*," the mother-land of the gods and of the ancestors of the Egyptians, where the god Osiris reigned supreme over the souls emancipated from the trammels of matter.

In the depths of the forests that cover the soil of Central America, lie hidden, under a cloak of verdure, the ruins of ancient cities. There, are to be seen the crumbling, awe-inspiring remains of grand old monuments; mementos of the power and civilization, of the scientific and intellectual attainments of the mighty races that erected them, and have disappeared forever in the abyss of time.

At Uxmal, one of these ancient great metropolis in Yucatan, there exists an artificial mound of peculiar construction.

The entire structure measured 29 metres (about 95 feet) in height; 66 metres (214 feet 6 inches) in length at the base, and 33 metres (107 feet 3 inches) in width. The lower part is formed of the frustum of an elliptical cone 14 metres (45 feet 6 inches) in height, divided into 7 gradients, each 2 metres high. On the upper plane of the frustum, which forms a terrace 35 metres long by 10 metres wide, are constructed the Sanctuary, or Holy of Holies, facing west, whose ground plan is made in the shape of a cross with a double set of arms; and a truncated rectangular pyramid 6 metres high, the upper plane of which supports the crowning edifice 6 metres high, 29 metres long and 7 metres wide.

This building emblem of the "Lands of the West," is composed of three separate apartments 2m. 25c. wide, having originally no communication with each other. Holes have been bored in the partition walls that have much weakened the construction; for what purpose it is difficult to surmise, unless it be for the love of destruction.

The rooms at the extremities are of the same size, 5m. 50c. (about 17 feet 10 inches) long, while the middle chamber is 7m. 25c. in length. The door of this chamber faced west, and led, by means of a small stair, to a terrace formed by the roof of the sanctuary.

From there the learned priests and astronomers, elevated above the mists of the plains below, could without hindrance follow the course of the celestial bodies, in the clear cloudless skies of Yucatan, where at times the atmosphere is so pure and transparent that stars are clearly visible to the naked eye, that require the aid of the telescope to be seen in other countries.

The doors of the other rooms faced East. The ceilings, like those of all the apartments in the monuments of Yucatan and Central America, form a triangular arch. This shape was adopted by the builders, not because they were ignorant of how to construct circular arches—since they erected edifices roofed with domes, but in accordance with certain esoteric teachings pertaining to the mysteries and relating to the mystic numbers 3.5.7.

This kind of arch is also found in the ancient tombs of Chaldea, at Mughier—in the center of the great pyramid of Ghizeh, in Egypt—in the most ancient monuments of Greece, as the treasure room at Mikéné, in the tombs of Etruria and other places.

Here, again, we learn from the book of Henoch, that the subterranean building that he constructed in the land of Canaan in the bowels of the mountain, with the help of his son Mathusalath, was in imitation of the nine vaults that were shown to him by the Deity, each apartment being roofed with an arch, the apex of which formed a key-stone with mirific characters inscribed on it. Each of the nine letters, we are told, represented one of the nine names traced in characters emblematical of the attributes of Deity. Henoch then constructed two triangles of the purest gold, and traced two of the mysterious characters on each. One he placed in the deepest arch; the other he entrusted to Mathusalath, *to whom he communicated important secrets.*

The triangular arches appear, therefore, as landmarks of one and the same doctrine, practised in remote times, in India, Egypt, Chaldea, Greece, Etruria and Central America.

In the ceilings of the rooms situated at the north and south extremities of the building are carved in peculiar and regular order, in deep intaglio, semispheres, ten centimeters in diameter, intended to represent the stars that at night so beautify the firmament. Inside of the triangle formed at each end of said rooms by the converging lines of the arch are also several of these semispheres—those in the north room form a triangle; while those in the south room, five in number, figure a trapezium; with one of these half spheres in the middle.

The middle chamber is now devoid of decorations of any sort. Its length, *seven* meters, is today the only vestige which remains to indicate that in it, in former times, were practised rites and ceremonies pertaining to the third degree of initiation. This chamber could be reached by walking on the narrow terrace round the building; but I feel certain that those whose privilege it was to assemble within its walls, got to it from the west side.

There was a stairway nine metres wide, beautifully ornamented, leading from the court yard adjoining the priests' palace, to the entrance of the sanctuary. Thence another small stairway 2m. 40c. wide, situated on the north side of the sanctuary, led to the upper terrace, to the roof of that monument, and to the middle chamber. The access to the north and south rooms was by a grand stairway of ninety-six steps, each 20cm. high, that led to the upper terrace surrounding the whole edifice. This stairway, situated on the east side of the mound, is fourteen metres (45 feet 6 inches) wide, and, like that on the east side, so steep as to require no little practice and care to ascend and descend its narrow steps with comparative safety and ease.

A few centimetres above the lintel of the entrance to the sanctuary is a cornice that surrounds the whole edifice. On it are sculptured symbols, many times repeated. On the under part of this cornice are small rings cut in the stone, from which curtains were suspended, to hide the Holy of Holies from profane gaze.

The exterior of the monument was once upon a time ornamented with elaborate and beautifully executed sculptures, which have now, in great part, disappeared. Still those that adorn the exterior walls of the sanctuary, remain as specimens of the beautiful handiwork and of the great skill of the artists; whilst the exquisite architectural proportions of the whole edifice bespeak the mathematical and other scientific attainments of the architects who planned the building and superintended its erection.

The ornaments that cover these walls are remarkable in more than one sense. They are not only inscriptions in the Maya language, written in characters identical with, and having the same meaning and value as those carved on the temples of Egypt; but among them are symbols known to have belonged to the ancient sacred mysteries of the Egyptians, and to modern Free Masonry. In August 1880, among the débris, at the foot of the mound just described, I found pieces of what once had been the statue of a priest. The part of the statue, from the waist to the knee, particularly attracted my attention. Over his dress the personage wore an apron with an extended hand. A symbol that will easily be recognized by members of the masonic fraternity.

We must not forget that Plato informs us that the priests of Egypt assured Solon, when he visited them 600 years before the Christian era, that all communications between their people and the inhabitants of the "Lands of the West" had been interrupted for 9,000 years, in consequence of the great cataclysms, during which, in one night, the large island of Atlantis disappeared, submerged under the waves of the ocean. Are we not then right if we surmise that the monuments of Mayax existed 11,500 years ago, and that mysteries, similar to those of Egypt, were celebrated in them? To support that belief we have the symbols already mentioned as existing in the chambers, the construction of the chambers themselves, the sculptures carved on the cornice that surrounds the sanctuary, representing cross bones and skeletons, with arms and hands uplifted, tokens that many of the Masons again cannot fail to recognize; besides other emblems that I will endeavor to explain, which exist on the walls of the residence of the priests, an edifice adjoining that temple. This may be considered the oldest known edifice in the world consecrated to secret rites and ceremonies; and its builders the founders of the sacred mysteries, that were transported from Mayax to India, Chaldea, Egypt, Etruria, by colonists or missionaries.

What the ceremonies of initiation were among the Mayas, it is difficult to surmise at present, all their books, except four that still exist, having been destroyed by the monks who came with the Spanish adventurers, or soon after the conquest.

But they must have been similar to the rites of initiation practiced by the *Quiches*, a branch of the Maya nation, at *Xibalba*, a place in the heart of the mountains of Guatemala. We learn from the *Popol-Vuh*, sacred book of the

Quiches, that the applicants for initiation to the mysteries were made to cross two rivers, one of mud, the other of blood, before they reached the four roads that led to the place where the priests awaited them. The crossing of these rivers was full of dangers that were to be avoided. Then they had to journey along the four roads, the white, the red, the green and the black, that led to where the council, composed of *twelve* veiled priests, and a wooden statue dressed and wearing ornaments as the priests, awaited them. When in presence of the council, they were told to salute the King; and the wooden statue was pointed out to them. This was to try their discernment. Then they had to salute each individual, giving his name or title without being told; after which they were asked to sit down on a certain seat. If, forgetting the respect due to the august assembly, they sat as invited, they soon had reason to regret their want of good breeding and proper preparation, for the seat, made of stone, was burning hot. Having modestly declined the invitation, they were conducted to the "Dark house," where they had to pass the night, and submit to the second trial. Guards were placed all round, to prevent the candidates from holding intercourse with the outer world. Then a lighted torch of pine wood and a cigar were given to each. These were not to be extinguished. Still they had to be returned whole at sunrise, when the officer in charge of the house came to demand them. Woe to him who allowed his torch and cigar to get consumed! Terrible chastisements, death, even, awaited him.

Having passed through this second trial successfully, the third was to be suffered in the "House of Spears." There, they had to produce four pots of certain rare flowers, without communicating with any one outside, or bringing them at the time of their coming; and had also to defend themselves, during a whole night, against the attacks of the best spearmen, selected for the purpose, one for each candidate. Coming out victorious at dawn, they were judged worthy of the fourth trial. This consisted in being shut for a whole night in the "Ice house," where the cold was intense. They had to prevent themselves from being overcome by the cold and frozen to death.

The fifth ordeal was not less terrible. It consisted in passing a night in company with wild tigers, in the "Tiger house," exposed to be torn to pieces, or devoured alive, by the ferocious animals. Emerging safe from the den, they had to submit to their sixth trial in the "Fiery house." This was a burning furnace where they had to remain from sunset to sunrise. Coming out unscorched, they were ready for the seventh trial, said to be the most severe of all, in the "House of the bats." The sacred book tells us it was the house of *Camazotz*, the "God of the bats," full of death-dealing weapons, where the God himself, coming from on high, appeared to the candidates and beheaded them, if off their guard.

Do not these initiations vividly recall to mind what Henoch said he saw in his visions? That blazing house of crystal, burning hot and icy cold—that place where were the bow of fire, the quiver of arrows, the sword of fire—that other where he had to cross the babbling stream, and the river of fire—and those extremities of the Earth full of all kinds of huge beasts and birds—or the habitation where appeared one of great glory sitting upon the orb of the sun—and, lastly, does not the tamarind tree in the midst of the earth, that he was told was the Tree of Knowledge, find its simile in the calabash tree, in the middle of the road where those of Xibalba placed the head of Hunhun Ahpu, after sacrificing him for having failed to support the first trial of the initiation? Even the title *Hach-mac*, "the true, the very man," of the high priest in Mayax, that we see over the bust of High Pontiff, prince *Cay Canchi*, son of King *Can* at Uxmal, recalls that of the chief of the Magi at Babylon.

These were the awful ordeals that the candidates for initiation into the sacred mysteries had to pass through in Xibalba. Do they not seem an exact counterpart of what happened, in a milder form at the initiation into the Eleusinian mysteries? and also the greater mysteries of Egypt, from which these were copied? Does not the recital of what the candidates to the mysteries in Xibalba were required to know, before being admitted, in order to distinguish the wooden statue pointed out to them as the King from the veiled Brothers; to avoid seating themselves on a burning hot stone seat; to keep lighted the torch and cigar and prevent them from being consumed;

to produce the flowers asked from them while isolated from the world in a guarded chamber; to defend themselves from the attacks of dexterous spearmen; to protect themselves against the intense cold of the "Ice house;" to remain unhurt amidst wild tigers; or unscorched in the middle of a burning furnace; recall to mind the wonderful similar feats said to be performed by the *Mahatmas*, the Brothers in India, and of several of the passages of the book of Daniel, who had been initiated to the mysteries of the Chaldeans or Magi which, according to Eubulus were divided into three classes or genera, the highest being the most learned?

Will it be said that the mysteries were imported from Egypt or Chaldea or India, or Phœnicia to America? Then I will ask when? By whom? What facts can be adduced to sustain such assertion? Why should the words with which the priest at the conclusion of the ceremonies in the Eleusinian mysteries, and the Brahmins at the end of their religious ceremonies, dismiss the assistants, be Maya instead of Greek or Sanscrit words? Is it not probable that the dismissal continued to be uttered in the language of those who first instituted and taught the ceremonies and rites of the mysteries to the others? That sacred mysteries have existed in America from times immemorial, there can be no doubt. Even setting aside the proofs of their existence, that we gather from the monuments of Uxmal, and the description of the trials of initiation related in the sacred book of the Quiches, we find vestiges of them in various other countries of the Western Continent.

Garcilasso de la Vega informs us that in Peru, it was illicit for any one not belonging to the nobility to acquire learning. There again, as in Egypt, in Chaldea, Etruria, India, Mayax, science was the privilege of the priests and kings. The sacerdotal class held the pre-eminence. Sacerdotal orders were conferred only upon young men who had given proofs of sufficiency for such important office; and before they could be received into the Society of the *Amautas* or wise men, which was considered a great honor, they had to submit to very severe ordeals. The rites and ceremonies of initiation were imported in Peru by the ancestors of Manco Capac, the founder of the Inca dynasty, who were colonists from Central America, as we learn from an unpublished MS., written by a Jesuit father, Rev. Anello Oliva, at the beginning of the year 1631, in Lima; and now in the library of the British Museum in London. The name *Quichua*, of the general language of Peru, points directly to the *Quiches* as the branch of the Maya nation that carried civilization to that country.

If from South America we go to New Mexico, there we find the Zuñis, and other Pueblo Indians. Having preserved their independence by shaking off at an early period the yoke of the Spaniards, they have been little influenced, if at all, by the civilization of the Europeans, and live today as their ancestors did many centuries back; preserving with great care, not only the purity of their language, which they teach their children to speak correctly, but their customs, traditions, and ancient religious rites and observances.

Mr. Frank Cushing, who was commissioned by the Smithsonian Institution, at Washington, to make a study of their customs and manners, has been adopted by the tribe, and has now become one of their most influential chiefs. Among the many interesting things discovered by him, not the least is the existence of *twelve sacred orders*, with their priests, their initiations, their sacred rites, as carefully guarded as the secrets of the ancient sacred mysteries to which they bear great resemblance. He has been initiated into many of them, having had to submit to ordeals almost as severe as those of Xibalba from which no doubt they are derived, having been brought among them by Maya colonists and afterward Nahualt invaders. The Nahualts invaded and for a long time held sway over Mexico and some of the northern portions of Central America. The aborigines of those countries at last expelled them from their territories, when they scattered in all directions, about the beginning of the Christian era. Some reached as far north as the gulf of California and Arizona. The Yaqui Indians, neighbors of the Mayos, and who inhabit the countries watered by the rivers Yaqui and Mayo in Sonora, are descendants of a Nahualt tribe, from which in all probability, the adjoining nations, the inhabitants of the seven cities of Cibola, the Zuñis among them, learned many of their religious practices; and the institution of the *twelve* sacred orders, that recall the *twelve* priests who presided at the initiation into the sacred mysteries at Xibalba.

Seeking for the origin of the institution of the sacred mysteries, of which Masonry seems to be the great-grandchild, following their vestiges from country to country, we have been brought over the vast expanse of the blue sea, to this western continent, to these mysterious "Lands of the West" where the souls of all good men, the Egyptians believed, dwelt among the blessed. It is, therefore, in that country, where Osiris was said to reign supreme, that we may expect to find the true signification of the symbols held sacred by the initiates in all countries, in all times, and which have reached us, through the long vista of ages, still surrounded by the veil, well-nigh impenetrable, of mystery woven round them by their inventors. My long researches among the ruins of the ancient temples and palaces of the Mayas, have been rewarded by learning at the fountain-head the esoteric meaning of some at least of the symbols, the interpretation of which has puzzled many a wise head—the origin of the mystification and symbolism of the numbers 3, 5, and 7.

Whoever has read history knows that in all nations, civilized as well as uncivilized, from the remotest antiquity, the priests have claimed learning as the privilege of their caste, bestowed upon them by special favor of the Ruling Spirit of the universe. For this reason they have zealously kept from the gaze of other men their intellectual treasures, and surrounded them with the veil of mystery. They have carefully hid all their discoveries, scientific or artistic, under the cover of symbols, reserving their esoteric or secret meaning for the initiated; giving to the people only such exoteric or public explanation of them as best suited their purpose. They put into practice the principle, that "It was necessary to keep the discoveries of the philosophers in the works of art or nature from those unworthy of knowing them," enunciated by the erudite and celebrated English monk Roger Bacon, one of the most learned men of his time, who was confined during many years in a prison cell by his ignorant brethren on account of his great erudition. This same principle is yet closely adhered to by the Brahmins, the Buddhist priests of Thibet, the Adepts of India, and I might add the Jesuits among the

Christians, although they are very inferior in knowledge to the others; the secrecy they have observed for centuries, and do still observe, being their best guarantee of power and honor.

Judging from the numerous devices and emblems that formed the ornamentation of the temples and palaces in the ancient ruined cities of Yucatan, the priests of Mayax seem to have been as addicted to symbology as their congeners in India, Egypt, Chaldea and other countries. Among these devices and symbols, several belong clearly to their sacred mysteries.

The study of the relics of ancient Maya civilization has made manifest to my mind the source of many of the primitive traditions of mankind, which have reached us through the sacred books of the Hindoos, the Chaldeans, the Egyptians, and the Jews. These, having received them from both the Chaldees and the Egyptians, have consigned the relation in the Pentateuch, a book long attributed to Moses, but now believed by Matthew Henry and other commentators, who pride themselves upon their orthodoxy, to have been written in times subsequent to the foundation of the Hebrew monarchy. Might it not be possible that, in Mayax also, could be found the origin of the mystification of the numbers 3, 5, and 7, regarded as mystic by all civilized nations of antiquity all over the earth?

Surely this mystification must have originated with one of these nations and been carried to the others either by colonists, missionaries, or travelers. It is not admissible, or even presumable, that the same idea and mysticism has been attached to these numbers by all these different peoples without being communicated from one to another. Such abstruse speculations respecting the ontological properties of numbers can not be ascribed to the first workings of the human mind in its incipient steps toward intellectual development. In its awakening, human intellect, still unable to comprehend the causes of the natural phenomena that take place, as everyday occurrences, in the material existence of man, does not soar in the elevated regions of metaphysics or of philosophical and abstract theories. Do we not see, even in our midst, that men who live in ignorance ascribe the manifestations of the powers of nature to unseen, mighty beings, of whom they continually stand in awe; to whom they tribute homage, and address prayers filled with the superstitious fears that these fancies of their untutored imagination inspire in them? Abstract conceptions, numerical combinations, metaphysical speculations, philosophical hypothesis, are productions of highly cultivated intelligences, of minds accustomed to reason on causes and effects, to deduce things unseen from things seen.

The mysticism with which these numbers have been invested, their symbolization in the sacred mysteries, must have had its origin in material causes, palpable to physical senses, the memory of which became lost in the course of ages, altered by being transported among peoples living far away from the nation that conceived the idea, by passing from mouth to mouth, in the secrecy of initiations, generation after generation. The idea of a sole and omnipotent Deity, who created all things, seems to have been the universal belief in early ages, among all the nations that had reached a high degree of civilization. This was the doctrine of the Egyptian priests. They called the Divine Intelligence *Kneph*, and placed him above and apart from the Triads. Damascius, an eclectic philosopher, who taught in the schools of Athens, about the year 526 of the Christian era, in his "Treatise on Principles," says that "they asserted nothing of the first principle of all things, but celebrated it as a thrice unknown darkness, transcending all intellectual perception." Proclus, platonic philosopher, director of the school of Athens in 450 after Christ, says: "the Demiurgos or Creator is triple, and the three intellects are the three kings, he who exists, he who possesses, he who beholds." These three intellects, therefore, he supposes to be the Demiurge; the same as the *three kings* of Plato, and as the three whom Orpheus celebrates under the names of Phænes, Ouranos, and Kronos, kings of the great "Saturnian continent," in the Atlantic ocean.

In Chaldea, the twin sister of Egypt, daughter of *Poseidon*, king of the "Lands beyond the sea" and Lybia, we find that notwithstanding the apparent polytheistic character which, from the earliest times, religion had assumed, it was possible for the priests and learned men, if we give credence to Pythagoras, Democritus, and other philosophers, to account by esoteric explanation for the multiplicity of their gods, resolving them into the powers of nature, thus reconciling the whole scheme with monotheism. In fact, above and apart from the personages which peopled their Pantheon and were reverenced with equal respect by kings and people, they recognized a superior deity, Ra, so far removed from their first triad, that they did not know how to worship it. The meaning of the name *RA* seems to have been unknown to the historians. They only assert that it means God emphatically; but its origin still remains a mystery. In Egypt they gave that name to the "Sun" particularly, as the fount of all things, the life-giver and sustainer of all that exists on earth. *LA*, in the Maya language, means "that which has existed forever. The eternal truth."

So it is evident that the ancient Chaldeans recognized a supreme being, a divine essence, *Ra*, to which the Triads were subordinate.

The same conceptions about Deity existed in India from the remotest antiquity. H. T. Colebrooke, in his notice on "the Sacred Books of the Hindoos" says: "In the last part of the *Niroukta*, dedicated exclusively to the divinities, it is thrice affirmed that there are only *three gods*; and that these three gods designate *one sole deity*. The gods are *three* only, whose mansions are the Earth, the intermediate regions and heavens; that is the fire, the air, and the sun; but *Pradjapati*, the Lord of all creatures, is their collective God. In fact there is but one God, the "great Soul" *Maha-atma*. It is called the "*SUN*," because the sun is the soul of all beings, of all that moves, and of all that does not move. The other gods are only parts or fractions of his person." The belief in a Triune God has also existed from very early ages among the Chinese philosophers. Lo-pi, a Chinese writer, who flourished toward the eleventh century of the Christian era, during the Songs dynasty, explaining certain passages of the *Hi-Tse*, says: That the "Great Term," is "the Great Unit" and the great Y. That the Y has neither body or shape. That all that has body and shape was made by that which has no body or shape. Tradition recounts that the "Great Term" or the "Great Unit" comprehends three; that one is three and three are one.

Hiu-Chin, who lived under the dynasty of the Hans, is the author of a Chinese dictionary called *Choueven* in which he has preserved many ancient traditions. He wrote about the beginning of the Christian era. Explaining the character Y he says: In the first beginning reason subsisted in unity. Reason made and divided Heaven and Earth; converted and perfected all things. And *Tao-Tse*, a contemporary of Confucius, who wrote the *Tao-te-King*, a book reputed very profound, said more than five hundred years before Christ: "That reason, *Tao*, produced one. That one produced two, that both produced three; and that three had produced all things." All early writers who have given an account of the religion of the ancient Peruvians, tell us that they worshiped a mighty unseen being who they believed had created all things, for which reason they called him *Pacha-camac*. He, being incomprehensible, they did not represent under any shape or figure, although they raised a magnificent temple in his honor on the sea coast that rivaled in wealth and splendor those dedicated to the Sun at Titicaca and Cuzco. We are also informed that He stood at the head of a trinity composed of Himself—*Pacha-camac*—*Con*—and *Uiracocha*.

In this conception of a Supreme Being, Creator of all things, we see reflected the teachings of the *Popol-vuh*, Sacred book of the Quiches, in which we read, "that all that exists is the work of *Tzakol*—the Creator— who by his will caused the Universe to spring into existence, and whose names are *Bitol*—the maker—*Alom*—the engenderer—*Qaholom*—He who gives being."

The fact that the same doctrine of a Supreme Deity composed of three parts distinct from each other, yet forming one, was universally prevalent among the civilized nations of America, Asia and the Egyptians, naturally leads to the inference that at some time or other, communications and relations more or less intimate have existed between them. They must, then, have imparted their traditions, metaphysical speculations, and intellectual attainments one to another.

In fact, all historians agree with Philostratus and admit that commercial intercourse did exist between Egypt and India. Nay more, Eusebius asserts that in the reign of Memnon, king of Ethiopia, a body of Ethiopians from the countries about the Indus river migrated and settled in the valley of the

Nile. And the many Chinese bottles, with inscriptions in that language, found in the tombs of Thebes, prove, beyond the least doubt, that communications have existed between the inhabitants of China and the Egyptians in times very remote, as is conjectured from the inferior quality of the bottles, that some seem to believe were manufactured before the art of making objects of porcelain reached the high degree of perfection to which it attained afterward.

On the other hand, the vase with Chinese inscriptions found by Dr. Schliemann in the lowest stratum of his excavations at Hissarlik, inscriptions that were partly deciphered by the eminent indianist Mr. Emile Burnouf and afterward thoroughly interpreted by the great Chinese scholar Fi-Fangpao, when ambassador at Berlin, and proved to mention the fact of the vase having contained samples of Chinese gauze, shows that active commercial intercourse was carried on by the Chinese with Greece and Asia Minor even before the siege of Troy.

These conceptions concerning the Triune God have come down through the vista of ages, to the present day, preserved in the works of the philosophers, and are still held sacred by many among Christians and Brahmins. But we do not learn from their sacred books where, when or how said doctrine originated. Whatever may have been the source from which it sprang, it is certain that the priests and learned men of Egypt, Chaldea, India, or China, if they still knew the true history of its origin at the time they wrote, kept it a profound secret, and imparted it only to a few select among those initiated in the sacred mysteries.

We need not seek for information among the fathers of the Christian Church, for they are as silent as the tomb on the subject. They admitted into their tenets the notion of a Triune God as taught by the pagan philosophers, and appropriated it, as they have many other of their teachings and theories, without knowing, without inquiring, concerning their origin. The councils pronounced them revelations from on high; unfathomable mysteries not to be investigated; and imposed them as dogmas, to be implicitly believed, with blind faith, as they are today, by the followers of the Romish Church.

Through their adherents the idea of the three persons in the Godhead has found its way into Free Masonry, and on the columns that adorn the temple, in the working of one of the degrees, we read these inscriptions: "*In the name of the holy and indivisible Trinity*;" and further down, "*We have the happiness to dwell in the pacific unity of the sacred numbers.*"

To those initiated to the lesser mysteries the doctrine was presented under the garb of the complicated metaphysical speculations with which it has reached us. Such explanations of the symbolical nature of the mystic numbers were given to them so as to make it well-nigh impossible to obtain a fair understanding of their purport. By the perusal of the extracts just quoted it is easy to see that all the reasonings concerning the mystic value of number 3 and its relations to a Supreme Deity are mere fancies of the imagination, vague speculations, fallacious cavils; meaningless for practical and inquiring minds. So far as explaining the nature of the Deity all philosophers agree in admitting that it transcends the intelligence of man since man is finite; and what is finite will never be able to comprehend that which is infinite.

Some of the Greek philosophers reflected in their teachings, as well as in their writings, the doctrines they had learned from their teachers, the priests of Heliopolis, Memphis and Thebes. From them we may gather a glimmer of dim light pointing toward the origin of the symbolization of the numbers. We have said that Proclus asserts that the three component parts of the triple deity were three intellects or *three Kings*—a fact corroborated by Plato, who also had been admitted to the mysteries, and by Orpheus, who celebrated these *three Kings*, in the ceremonies instituted by him, that Herodotus says were identical with the Egyptian mysteries.

Pythagoras, who had received his knowledge of the numbers and their meaning from the Egyptians, taught his disciples that God was number and harmony. He caused them to honor numbers and geometrical diagrams with the names of the gods. The Egyptians likened nature to the equilateral triangle, the most perfect and beautiful of all triangles; and according to Servius, assigned the perfect number 3 to the great God.

The Chaldees symbolized the Eusoph or great light, by an equilateral triangle; and in the *Sri-Santara* or cosmogonical diagram of the Hindoos, which has served as model for many of their temples, the nameless, the great *Aum* that dwells in the infinite, is figured as an equilateral triangle. The Egyptians held the equilateral triangle as the symbol of "Nature" beautiful and fruitful. In the hieroglyphs it was the emblem of worship. We see, over the main altar, in all the ancient Catholic churches, the representation of an equilateral triangle containing the all-seeing eye of Osiris, as symbol of Deity. The same emblem is familiar also to those who visit masonic lodges as one under which is figured the "Great Architect of the Universe."

If from those countries that we have been accustomed to consider as the "Old World," and guided by the three words of dismissal used by the Brahmins, and the officiating priests of Eleusis, at the closing of their religious ceremonies, words we have shown to belong to the Maya language, we carry our inquiries into the "Lands of the West," there again we will find that the triangle was also symbolical among the Mayas and their neighbors.

We see it in the position of the three semispheres carved, as already said, at each end of the northern chamber of the building above the sanctuary at Uxmal. We next meet with it in the triangular arches that form the ceilings of the apartments in all the temples and palaces, in fact in all the edifices of Mayax, as well as in those of Palenque and other localities of Central America.

The general plan of these edifices is the same everywhere; not because they were built by the same architects, or at the same period, but because their construction was in accordance with certain teachings pertaining to the mysteries. In all the buildings, whatever their size, the ground plan was in the shape of an oblong square , that is of their letter M, pronounced *Ma*. Ma is the contraction of *Mam*, the ancestor, as they denominated the Earth, and by extension the Universe. *Ma* is also the radical of *Ma-yax*, the name of the Yucatecan peninsula, in ancient times, whose shape, no doubt, suggested that of the letter *M*, both to the Mayas and to the Egyptians. In fact, in Egypt and in Mayax, the figure in the hieroglyphs, stands for Earth and Universe. It will be noticed by examining their plans, that this was also the shape of the apartments in the temples and palaces of Chaldea, of Egypt and Greece; that of the tombs of the Etruscans; hence, no doubt, was assigned to the masonic lodges in our days.

The triangular ceiling in those countries, and there is no reason for doubting that it was the same in the "Lands of the West," was symbolical of the Triune God, the Ruling Spirit of the Universe, supposed to reside in the heavens, above all things. (This accounts for the constellations of the firmament being represented on the ceilings).

According to Zoroaster, He is the fire, the sun, the light; that the later Platonists have described as power, intellect, soul, or spirit; and the ancient theologians, who invoked the sun in their mysteries, according to Macrobius, as power of the world, light of the world, spirit of the world; that Plutarch gives as intelligence, matter, kosmos, beauty, order, the world; of these three he says, "universal nature may be considered to be made up, and there is reason to conclude that the Egyptians were wont to liken this nature to what they called the most beautiful and perfect triangle."

It will be noticed that the geometrical figure formed at the ends of each of these apartments, by the lines of the ceilings, sides, and floor, is a pentagon, symbol of the mystic number 5 whose name, *penta*, in Greek also conveys the idea of Universe; whilst *Ho* in Maya, meaning 5, is also the radical of *Hool*, the head, hence the Deity.

Then, lastly, the number of planes forming the rooms—the two of the ceilings, the two of the sides, the two of the ends, and that of the floor—*seven* in all, shows conclusively not only why the builders adopted the triangular arch instead of the circular, but also that the plan of their buildings was conceived in strict adherence to the mystic numbers 3, 5, 7, or their multiples, as we see by the height of the pyramids; the number of courses of the stones forming the walls; that of the terraces on which the temples stood; that of the degrees of the stairs by which they were reached.

Only two edifices of different construction have been found among the ancient cities of the Mayas. One, now completely ruined, having been shattered by a thunderbolt in 1848, was in Mayapan. That place was destroyed, according to Bishop Landa, in the year 1446 of the Christian era, by the lords and nobles of the country, to put an end to the dynasty of the Cocomes that governed with tyrannical rule. The other, still standing, although much injured by the action of time and vegetation, is to be seen in the most ancient city of Chichen. These buildings were consecrated to the study of astronomy; no doubt also to the performance of certain religious ceremonies connected with the worship of the sun, moon, and other celestial bodies. They were circular; their ground plan formed three concentric circles representing the Zodiac, and their vertical section, in its general outlines, conveys to the mind that, in their inward or esoteric construction placed before the eyes of the masses yet hidden from them, the architect wished to represent the figure of the mastodon, which was venerated by the people as image of Deity on Earth—probably because this pachyderm was the largest and most powerful creature that lived in the land.

Among the ornaments which beautified one of the seven turrets that adorned the south façade of the north wing of the ancient palace of King *CAN*, and were dedicated to each of the seven members composing his family, on that set apart to commemorate the name of his eldest son Cay (Fish), the high pontiff, are seen these symbols:

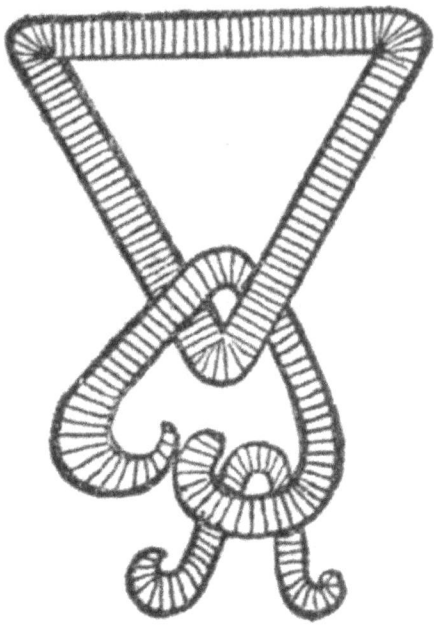

My knowledge of the symbols and sacred characters used by the learned priests of Mayax, in the mural inscriptions and ornaments of their temples and palaces, enables me to understand their exoteric meaning. The symbol above is composed of an equilateral triangle with the apex downward; through it passes a ribbon tied in a knot. The triangle seems here to represent the whole country, the "Lands of the West," composed of *three* great continents, "North and South America" of today, and "the great island," called Atlantis by Plato, that disappeared in the midst of an awful cataclysm, under the waves of the ocean, as described by the author of the Troano MS., who thus confirms the account of it given by the priests of Egypt, to Solon. The ribbon tied in a knot would indicate that the initiates, to whom the esoteric explanation of the symbol had been imparted, were bound to each other, to secrecy and to their oath. Its hidden meaning may have been that the equilateral triangle represented Deity ever watchful, always creating—Nature in which we move, and live and have our being, in which all things are bound.

The emblem above seems to have belonged more particularly to the highest degree of the sacred mysteries, since we find it among other symbols sculptured on the slabs that formed the external casing of the mausoleum raised to the memory of the high pontiff *Cay*. This second emblem is also a ribbon, tied up so as to form three loops, each occupying one angle of an oblong square, image of the Universe; the fourth angle being adorned with flat folds, that are emblematic of Mayax the seat or head of the government, so arranged as to form the steps—5 in number—of a throne. This accounts for their being placed at the upper angle. The *three* round loops are symbolical of the *three* great parts composing the "Lands of the West," that the Greek mythologists figured by the trident of Poseidon, their god of the sea. As to the sign, in Mayax as in Egypt, it was meant to represent the sun. It was placed in the middle of the square simply to signify that as the sun was the centre of the universe, the vivifying soul of all things, so his representative the "*Child of the Sun*," the high priest, was the light that illumined the secrets of the sacred mysteries by his wisdom; and whose knowledge made him the fit ruler of the country. Is also the first letter of the Maya and Egyptian alphabets, corresponding to our Latin letter A, initial of *Ah*, maya masculine article, denoting strength, power—*Ah* being likewise the first syllable of the word *Ahau* King.

We know as yet too little of the religious tenets of the ancient priesthood of Mayax, to venture upon an explanation. All we can assert positively is that number 7 was the particular appendage of the third degree of the mysteries. It was considered as endowed with great potentiality; was as Pythagoras says, the vehicle of life, containing soul and body.

What motives may have induced the founders of the mysteries in Mayax to select the numbers 3, 5, 7, as symbols of the various degrees into which they divided them, we can at present only surmise. It is probable that certain natural causes, or the commemoration of important events which had taken place in the life of the nation, or in that of the family of the founders of the dynasty that governed it, suggested their adoption. The fact is that the *seven* members of that family were collectively symbolized by the emblem of the *Ah-ac-Chapat* or *Seven* Headed Serpent. It is difficult to prognosticate if we shall ever obtain an insight into the secret teachings of the Mayas, even if we had access to their libraries; for it is to be presumed that they did not confide them to the papyrus of their books.

Landa, in his "Relation of the things of Yucatan," says: "The sons or the nearest relatives succeeded to the high priest in his dignity; with him was the key of their sciences, and in that they most concerned themselves, because it was the priests who gave advice to the lords and answered their queries.... It was the high priest who nominated the priests for cities or villages which had none, examined them as to their proficiency in sciences and ceremonies. He entrusted to them the things of their office, and bade them give good example to the people. The priests employed themselves in the service of the temple and in teaching their divers sciences, particularly how to write the books that contained them. They taught the sons of the other priests and the younger sons of the princes who were sent to them in their childhood, if they saw them inclined for that profession."

In order to understand the explanation of the possible origin of the mystification of the numbers 3, 5, and 7, it is necessary to know something of the people among whom it seems to have originated.

If we start from the mouths of the Mississippi River and travel due south, across the Gulf of Mexico, at a distance of exactly four hundred and eighty miles, we come to the northern coast of the Yucatecan Peninsula. Its northeasternmost point, Cape Catoche, is one hundred and twenty miles from Cape San Antonio, the western end of the island of Cuba. Yucatan divides the Gulf of Mexico from the Caribbean Sea. It is comprised between the 17° 30' and 21° 50' of latitude north, and the 88° and 91° of longitude west from the Greenwich meridian. Its length is, therefore, 260 miles from north to south, and its breadth 180 miles from east to west. The whole country is a fossiliferous limestone formation, elevated a few feet only above the sea; its maximum height in the interior being about 70 feet. Although its rocky surface, bare for the most part, is, in places only, covered with a few inches of tillable loam, formed by the detritus of the stones and the decomposition of vegetable matter, its soil is of surprising fertility.

The whole country is now covered with well-nigh impenetrable forests. A bird's eye view of it from the top of one of the lofty pyramids, that seem like light-houses in the midst of that ocean of foliage, impresses the beholder with the idea that he is looking on an immense sea of verdure having for boundary the horizon, and whose billows come to die, with gentle murmur, at the foot of the monument on which he stands. Not a hill, not a hillock even, breaks the monotony of the landscape, which is only relieved by clusters of palm trees that loom here and there, as islets, above the dead green level.

Anciently, this country, now well nigh depopulated, was thickly peopled by a highly civilized nation, if we are to judge by the great number of large cities whose ruins exist scattered in the midst of the forests throughout the country, and by the stupendous edifices, once upon a time temples of the gods, or palaces of the kings and priests, whose walls are covered with inscriptions, bas-reliefs, and other interesting sculptures that equal in beauty of design and masterly execution those of Egypt and Babylon.

The author of the Troano MS.—a very ancient treatise on geology, one of the four known books which escaped destruction at the hands of Bishop Landa and other fanatical Catholic monks who accompanied the Spanish invaders, when, after a struggle of twenty years, they at last, in 1541, became masters of the country—tells us that anciently the peninsula was called *MAYAX*; that is, the primitive land, the *terra firma*. It gave its name to the whole empire of the Mayas, that comprised all the countries known today as Central America, from the isthmus of Darien on the south, to that of Tehuantepec on the north. The site of the government was at Uxmal; but the great emporium of their arts and sciences, the heart, consequently, of that marvellous civilization, was at Chichen-Itza; that became a vast metropolis. In its temples pilgrims from all parts came to worship, and even offer their own persons as a sacrifice to the Almighty, by throwing themselves into the sacred well from which the city took its name. There also came the wise men from afar, to consult the *H-Menes*, learned priests, whose college still exists. Among these foreigners, were bearded men whose features vividly recall those of the Assyrians of old, and the Afghans of today.

From Chichen this great civilization seems to have extended its influence to the remotest parts of the Earth, and to have exercised its controlling power among far distant and heterogeneous nations. The fact is, that we meet with the name Maya in many countries of Asia, Africa, Europe, as well as of America, and always with the meaning of wisdom and power attached to it. Wherever we find it, there also are found vestiges of the language, of the customs, of the religion, of the cosmogonical and historical traditions of the people of Mayax. Many of these traditions have been recorded in the sacred books of various nations and have come to be regarded as the primitive history of mankind. To quote a few instances. The creation of the world, according to their conceptions, is sculptured, and forms an interesting tableau over the door-way, on the east façade of the palace at Chichen-Itza.

It might serve as illustration for the relation of the creation, as we read of it at the beginning of the first chapter of the Manava Dharma Sastra, or ordinances of Menu; a book compiled, says the celebrated indianist, H. T. Colebrooke, about 1300 years before the Christian era, and from other and more ancient works of the Brahmins. Said relation completed, however, by the narrative of the myth according to the Egyptians as told by Eusebius in his work *Evangelical Preparations*.

Effectively, in the tableau we see represented a luminous egg, emitting rays, and floating in the midst of the waters where it had been deposited by the Supreme Intelligence. In that egg is seated the Creator, his body painted blue, his loins surrounded by a girdle; he holds a sceptre in his left hand; his head is adorned with a plume of feathers; he is surrounded by a serpent, symbol of the Universe.

Porphyrius, speaking of Jupiter, the Creator in the Orphic mysteries, says, "the philosophers, that is the initiated, represented him as a man, *seated*, alluding to his immutable essence; *the upper part of the body naked*, because it is in its upper portions (in the skies) that the Universe is seen most uncovered; *clothed from the waist below* because the terrestrial things are those most hidden from view. *He holds a sceptre in his left hand* because the heart is on that side, and the heart is the seat of understanding that regulates all the actions of man."

And again, "the Egyptians call Kneph the intelligence, or creative power." *Kneph*, or be it *Kaneh*, seems a cognate of *can-hel*, a Maya word the meaning of which is serpent (dragon); they say that this god threw from his mouth an egg in which was produced another god called *Phtha*, (*Thah* is another Maya word, it means the worker—hence the Maker, the Creator); and Eusebius asserts, "That they represented Kneph, or the Efficient Cause, as a man of a blue color, with a girdle round his loins, a sceptre in his hand, a crown on his head, adorned with a plume of feathers; and that emblematically they figured him under the form of *a serpent*."

Will any one with common sense pretend that these conceptions concerning the Creator, we find not only identical, but expressed in like manner and with the same symbols, by the philosophers of India, of Egypt, and of Mayax, are mere coincidences? If they are not the result of hazard, they must have been conceived by the wise men of one of these countries, that, no doubt, in which the civilization was the oldest, and communicated to others; these, in turn, taught them to their neighbors, as we know the Egyptians did to the Greeks.

Again, we read in Genesis that at a very early period in man's history, a certain man murdered his brother through jealousy. The victim we are told was named *ABEL*, his murderer Cain.

No doubt the writer of the book simply repeated the story he had learned from the Egyptian priests, concerning the murder of Osiris (*in whose honor the mysteries were instituted*), by his brother *Set*, through jealousy; making such alterations in his narration as not to divulge the secrets he had sworn to keep.

If any of those initiated to the higher mysteries were still acquainted with the true history of the murder, they kept it a profound secret; and only gave of it such exoteric explanations as best suited their purpose. Very little can be learned from the ancient historians. Herodotus always excuses himself from speaking on the subject; although he asserts he is well acquainted with what pertained to the mysteries: and what we gather from the book of Plutarch, de *Iside et Osiride*, is a version invented to satisfy the initiates of the lower degrees. In it Osiris is represented as having become the culture hero of Egypt. After ascending the throne, having taught his subjects the arts of civilization, he undertook an expedition from Egypt, in order to visit and dispense the same benefits to the different countries of the world. He left his wife and sister Isis in charge of the affairs of the kingdom which she administered aided by the counsels of her friend and preceptor Thoth. Isis, being extremely vigilant, *Set*, her other brother, had no opportunity for making innovations in the government. Still he desired to sit on the throne. After the return of Osiris, he conspired against him and persuaded seventy-two other persons to join with him in the conspiracy, together with a certain queen of Ethiopia named *Aso* who happened to be in Egypt at the time. He invited his unsuspecting brother to a banquet, and caused a beautiful chest to be brought into the banqueting-room. It was much admired by all. He then, as if in jest, offered to give it to the person it fitted best. All tried getting into it one after another, but it did not fit any as well as Osiris when he in turn laid himself down in it. Then Set, aided by the conspirators, closed the lid and fastened it on the outside with nails.

This story of a brother being slain at the request of another brother, through jealousy, is also related in Valmiki's ancient Sanscrit poem, the "Ramayana." We are not informed by the author from where he obtained it; but the victim was called *BÂLI*, and *MAYA* is represented as being his enemy. The recital of this event being identical with that archived in the sculptures and mural paintings still existing on the walls of certain edifices at Chichen-Itza, and with the account of it recorded in the second part of the Troano MS. would seem to indicate that the relation of the fratricide was brought to India by some Maya traveler or missionary; or maybe by the colonists from Mayax that Valmiki tells us took possession of and settled, in very remote ages, in the countries, at the south of the Indo-Chinese peninsula, known today as *Dekkan*. They, of course, brought to their new home with the language and customs, the civilization, traditions, and folk-lore from the mother country. Among these the tradition that, in very ancient times, the son of one of their primitive rulers murdered his brother through jealousy, in order to possess himself of his wife, with whom he had fallen in love, and of the reins of the government.

In the inflated style of the Hindoo poets Valmiki recounts the murder of Bâli. The story is as follows. There were two princes named Bâli and Sougriva, sons of a king of the Monkey nation. After the death of their father, Bâli the eldest was called to the throne, being elected sole monarch and supreme lord by the people. A terrible feud had originated between

Bâli and Maya on account of a woman they both coveted. Maya challenged Bâli to mortal combat and allured him into an ambush. Bâli not returning after a time was believed to have succumbed, and his brother Sougriva ascended the throne. Bâli returned however, and finding his brother installed in his place accused him of treason in the council of the nobles and before the people. He charged him with causing the news of his death to be circulated in order to usurp the reins of the government. Then he banished him from court, sent him adrift without means, depriving him of his home, his wife and his social position.

Sougriva met Rama; besought his help to avenge his wrongs. Having received his promise to kill Bâli, strong in the protection of such an ally, he challenged his brother to mortal combat, although he knew that alone he was not a match for him. During the encounter that ensued, Rama who was present, seeing that Sougriva was being badly beaten, sent an arrow through the breast of Bâli and killed him. The last word of that prince to his slayer who was standing by him, were: "What glory dost thou expect to reap from the death thou hast given me whilst I was not even looking toward thee? Hidden thou hast wounded me in a cowardly manner while my attention was engrossed in that duel." *And so Bâli was treacherously slain.*

We learn from the sculptures and mural paintings that adorn the walls of the palaces at Chichen-Itza and Uxmal that king *Can* (Serpent) the founder, or maybe the restorer, of these ancient cities, had three sons whose names were *Cay* (Fish), *Aac* (Turtle), and *Coh* (Leopard), and two daughters, *Moo* (Macaw), and *Nicté* (Flower).

It was the law among the Mayas that the youngest of the brothers should marry the eldest of the sisters to insure the legitimate and divine descent of the royal family. This same custom of princes of royal blood marrying their sisters existed among the Egyptians from the earliest days, and it became in after times general; such alliance being considered fortunate. It also prevailed with the Ethiopians, the Greeks, those of Mesopotamia in the time of the patriarchs, the Peruvians, and many other nations. Prince *Coh* was a brave and successful warrior; at the head of his followers, whom he had often led to victory, he had conquered many nations and greatly added to the glory and extent of the Maya empire. Being the youngest of the brothers, he was the one who had to marry Moo, the eldest of the sisters. She, on her part, loved him dearly and was proud of his exploits. After the death of King Can, their father, the country was parcelled among his children. Moo became the queen of Chichen, and many of the lords swore allegiance to her. After her death she received the honors of apotheosis; became the goddess of fire, and was worshiped in a magnificent temple, built on the summit of a high and very extensive pyramid whose ruins are still to be seen in the city of Izamal.

Aac, the second son of king Can, was also in love with her. To his lot had fallen the ancient metropolis *Uxmal*, "the three times rebuilt." His headless and legless statue is still to be seen over the main entrance on the façade of the palace known as the "House of the Governor," at that place. The flayed bodies of his two brothers and his eldest sister are at his feet; their heads hang from the belt round his waist: and the ruins of his private residence, ornamented with turtles,—his totem—yet exist at the northwest corner of the second of the three terraces on which the palace is built. The law of the land and her own predilection for Coh were insurmountable barriers that prevented Aac from marrying Moo. He was not a warrior but a courtier. He spent his life in idleness amidst pleasures and frivolities. Still he was envious of the fame won by his younger brother; jealous of him because of the love of the people, and still more of that of his sister and wife. He allowed his evil passions to gain the mastery over his better feelings. He incited a conspiracy against the friends of his childhood, with the object of killing his own brother, to obtain forcible possession of the sister he so much coveted, seize the reins of the government, and become the supreme lord of the whole empire.

In the carvings on the wooden lintels over the entrance of Coh's funereal chamber, in the paintings that adorn its walls, and in which that part of the life of the personages concerned in these events is portrayed, Aac is represented full of wrath, holding three spears in his hand, engaged in a terrible altercation with Coh. From the sculptures that adorned his mausoleum we learn that he was murdered treacherously by being stabbed with a spear three times in the back; and the author of the Troano MS. in giving an account of that murder and its consequences, has recorded this fact and illustrated it in the first section of plate xiv., in the second part of his work. [When I disinterred his statue, I found in an urn his heart, partially cremated, and the flint head of the spear with which he was slain.] In one of the tableaux of the mural paintings the body of Coh, surrounded by his wife, his sister *Nicté*, his children and his mother, is being prepared for cremation; the heart and other viscera having been extracted to be preserved in urns. A similar custom prevailed among the Egyptians of high rank whose bodies were embalmed according to the most expensive process. The internal parts of the body having been removed, were cleansed, embalmed in spices and various substances, then deposited in four vases that were placed in the tomb with the coffin.

At the death of Coh the whole country became involved in a civil war. The conspirators, partisans of Aac, striving to seize the reins of the government, the friends of Prince Coh fighting to avenge his death and in defense of their queen. The goddess of war favored at times one party, then the other. Aac, in order to obtain the preponderance, had recourse to diplomacy. He renewed his suit for the hand of his sister. He sent messengers to her, with a present of fruits, begging her to accept his love now that she was free. The scene is vividly pictured in the mural paintings.

Queen Moo is represented seated in her house situated in the middle of a garden. At her feet, but outside of the house to indicate that she does not accept it, is a basket full of oranges. Her extended left hand shows that she declines to listen to the messenger who stands before her in an entreating posture, and that she scorns the love of Aac who is seen on a lower plane, making an obeisance. Over his head is a serpent, typical of his name, *Can*, looking as lovingly as a serpent can be made to look, at a *Macaw* perched on the top of a tree and above the figure of the queen whose totem it is. The tree is guarded by a monkey in a threatening attitude. This monkey here, as in Egypt the cynocephalus, is the emblem of the preceptor of *Moo*, symbol therefor of wisdom.

This tableau is most interesting and significant, since in it we have a natural explanation of the myth of the temptation of the woman by the serpent. Here we have the garden, the woman, the temptor, and the fruit. The story of this family incident passing from mouth to mouth, from generation to generation, from country to country, has become disfigured probably by peoples that did not hold woman in as high esteem, or did not honor her as much as the Mayas did. Perhaps, also, an old misanthropical bachelor, hater of the fair sex, wrote a distorted account of the tradition out of spite at having been jilted by his lady-love, and his version was accepted by the author of Genesis, if he himself did not make the alteration. The fact is that the author of the Troano MS.—(Plate xvii., part second) as the artist who painted the scene just described—asserts that she refused to listen to *Aac's* entreaties, in consequence of which the civil war continued. At last *Moo* and her followers succumbed. She fell into the hands of Aac who, after ill-treating her, put her to death together with *Cay* the high pontiff, his elder brother, who had sided with the queen of Chichen, with right and justice. In token of his victory, *Aac* caused his statue—the feet resting on the flayed bodies of his kin, their heads being suspended from his belt—to be placed over the main entrance of the royal palace at Uxmal, where, as I have said, its remains may be seen today.

I may add here in explanation of the tableau of the scene in the garden, that the present of a basket of oranges was the offer of marriage made by *Aac* to *Moo*. It is usual with the aborigines of Yucatan, that yet retain many of the customs of their forefathers, when a young man wishes to propose marriage to a girl to send by a friend as a present, a fruit, or flower, or sweetmeat. The acceptance of the present is the sign that the proposal of the suitor is admitted, and from that moment they are betrothed; whilst the refusal of the present means that he is rejected. A similar custom exists in Japan. When a young lady expects a proposal of marriage a convenient flower-pot is placed in a handy position on the window-sill. The lover plants a flower in it. If next morning the flower is watered he can present himself to his lady-love knowing that he is welcome. If on the contrary, the flower has been uprooted and thrown on the side-walk, he well understands he is not wanted.

The family name of the kings of Mayax was *Can* (serpent) as *Khan* is still the title of the Kings of Tartary and Burmah, and of the governor of provinces in Persia, Afghanistan and other countries in Central Asia. *Can* was therefore the family name of Aac. The meaning of the writer of Genesis when he says that the serpent spoke to the woman and seduced her with a fruit is now easily understood.

The account of the fratricide in Genesis, in the Ramayana, or in the papyri of Egypt, is nothing more or less, with a slight variance, than the story of the feuds of king Can's children. This story, treasured by the priests of Egypt and India, consigned in their sacred books and poems, has been handed down to us among the primitive traditions of mankind.

Nowhere, except in Mayax, do we find it as forming part of the history of the nation. Nowhere, except in Mayax, do we find the portraits of the actors in the tragedy. There, we not only see their portraits carved in bas-reliefs, on stone or wood, or their marble statues in the round, or represented in the mural paintings that adorn the walls of the funereal chamber built to the memory of the victim, but we discover the ornaments they wore, the weapons they used, nay, more, their mortal remains.

The following is the certificate of Charles O. Thompson, Principal and Professor of Chemistry at the Worcester Free Institute, who made the chemical analysis of part of the cremated remains found in the stone urn that was near the chest of the statue that occupied the centre of the mausoleum raised to the memory of the famous warrior Coh, twenty feet below the upper plane of the monument.

"Under microscope it presents a certain compactness and horny aspect characteristic of animal matter which has been charred in a close vessel, it loses 9 per cent. when dried at 100° and 9 per cent. more by combustion. After calcination, a dross and residue remains which contains 3 per cent. fenic oxide, a little alumina and much silica. Warm water exposed to action of residue shows traces of potash and soda.

"These results are consistent with the theory that the mass was once part of a human body which has been burned with some fuel."

There is a fact certainly worthy of notice, and this is that the names of the personages mentioned in the various accounts of the fratricide are precisely identical, or are words having the same signification. May not that be regarded as unimpeachable proof that they all refer to the same event?

No one who has any knowledge of philology will ever deny that A-bel—A-bal—Bal-*i*—*Balam* are identical words.

A, contraction of *Ah*, is the Maya masculine article, *the*. *Bal* is the radical of Bal*am*. Balam is for the superstitious aborigines, even today, the *Yumil Kaax*—the "Lord of the fields" the "*Leopard*" which they also call *Coh*—the totem of the victim of Aac is the leopard—and it is so represented in the bas-reliefs and sculptures.

In Egypt, the spotted skin of the leopard, usually without the head, but sometimes with it, was always suspended near the images and statues of Osiris. The skin of a leopard was worn as a mantle over the ceremonial dress of his priests.

Besides, when represented as King of the Amenti—of the "West"—the symbol of Osiris was always a crouching leopard with an open eye over it.

We must not lose sight of the fact that the leopard's skin worn by Nimrod and Bacchus was a sacred appendage to the Mysteries. It was used in the Eleusinian as well as in the Egyptian mysteries instituted in honor of Osiris. It is mentioned in the earliest speculations by the Brahmins on the meaning of their sacrificial prayers the *Aytareya Brahmana*, and is used in the *agnishtoma* the initiation rites of the *Soma* mysteries. When the neophyte is to be born again he is covered with a "leopard skin," out of which he emerges as from his mother's womb. A leopard skin is worn by the African warriors, who are so fortunate as to possess one, as a charm to render them invulnerable to spears according to the French traveler Paul du Chaillu.

It would seem as if the manner in which *Coh* met his death, by being stabbed with a spear, had been known to their ancestors, and that they imagined that wearing his totem would save them from being wounded with the same kind of weapon used in killing him. That the inhabitants of Africa had communications with those of the Western Continent there can be no doubt, since populations of black people existed on the isthmus of Panama and other localities at the time of the first arrival of the Spaniards; besides their pictures can be seen in the mural paintings at Chichen.

As to the name *Osir*, or be it *Ozil*, it would seem to be a nickname given to *Coh* on account of the great love his sisters, and the people in general, professed for him. *Ozil* is a Maya verb that means to desire vehemently. He, therefore, who was very much desired—dearly beloved.

Osiris in Egypt, *Abel* in Chaldea, *Bali* in India, are myths. *Coh*, in Mayax, is a reality—a warrior whose mausoleum I have opened; whose weapons and jade ornaments are in my possession; whose heart I have found, and a piece of which was analyzed by Professor Thompson; whose statue, with his name inscribed on the tablets occupying the place of the ears, I have unearthed, and which is now in the National Museum in the City of Mexico, one of the most precious relics in that institution, having been robbed from me, by force of arms, by the Mexican authorities.

Isis was the wife and sister of Osiris. The word *Isis* may simply be a dialectical mode of pronouncing the Maya word *iɔin* (idzin) *the younger sister*. Her headgear, as a goddess, was a vulture. That bird was her totem and the peculiar type of maternity.

Isis was often called the great mother-goddess *Mau*; a word certainly as suggestive of the name *Moo*, sister and wife of Coh and queen of Chichen, as the *vulture* is of the *Macaw*. It must not be forgotten that one of the titles of Isis was the *royal wife and sister*.

Authors, who of course know nothing of the facts in the ancient history of Mayax, revealed to me by the sculptures and the mural paintings of the temples and palaces of the Mayas, and contained in the pages of the Troano MS., do not believe that Osiris and his sister Isis were deified persons who had lived on earth, but fabulous beings, whose history was founded on metaphysical speculations, and adapted to certain phenomena of nature. But the primitive rulers of the Mayas, whose history is an exact counterpart of that of the children of *Seb* and *Nut*, were deified after their death and worshiped as gods of the elements. My object is not here to enter into long explanations on these historical disclosures. I refer the reader who wishes to know more of the subject to my work, "The Monuments of Mayax and their Historical Teachings."

As to the names *Cain, Set, Sougriva, Aac*, they all convey the idea of something belonging to or having affinity with water.

Cain, by apocope, gives *Cay*, the Maya word for "fish."

Set is a cognate word of the Maya *Ze*, to ill-treat with blows. Can a name be more appropriate to designate one who has killed his brother with three thrusts of his spear; and his sister by kicking her to death, as *Aac* is represented doing by the author of the Troano MS.?

Set, after being treated with the same honor as the other members of the family of Seb, came to be regarded as the Evil principle and was called

Nubti, that is, according to the Maya language, the *adversary*, from *nup* adversary and *ti* for. He also was the Sun God, the enemy of the serpent. Here again we have a most singular resemblance, to say the least. *Aac*, in the sculptures of Mayax, is always pictured surrounded by the sun as his protecting genius; while the serpent, emblem of the country, always shields *Coh* and his sister-wife within its folds. The escutcheon of the city of Uxmal shows that the title of that metropolis was the "Land of the Sun." In the bas-reliefs of the queen's chamber at Chichen, the followers of *Aac* are seen to render homage to the *Sun*; the friends of *Moo* to the serpent. So in Mayax as in Egypt, the *Sun* and the *Serpent* were inimical. In Egypt this enmity was a myth; in Mayax a dire reality.

The hippopotamus and the crocodile were emblems of Set. Plutarch says "that at Hermopolis there was a statue of Set, which was a hippopotamus with a hawk upon its back fighting with a serpent." Both the hippopotamus and the crocodile are amphibious animals, having consequently much affinity with water.

Aac, in Maya, is the name for the turtle, also an amphibious animal.

The name Sougriva, of the brother of Bâli, is a word composed of three Maya primitives, *zuc, lib, ha*, *zuc*, quiet, tranquil; *lib*, to ascend, and *ha*, water—"He who tranquilly rises on the water" as the turtle does.

The universal deluge is another tradition of the early days that was credited by certain civilized nations of antiquity.

The Egyptian priests who, from times immemorial, had kept in the archives of the temples a faithful account of all events worthy of being remembered, derided the Greek philosophers when they spoke of the deluge of Deucalion and the destruction of the human race. Their answer was that as they had been preserved from it the inundation could not have been universal; they even added that the Hellenes were childish in attaching so much importance to that event, as there had been several other local catastrophes resembling it. They told Solon that the greatest cataclysm on record in their books was that during which Atlantis disappeared under the waves of the ocean, in one day and night, in consequence of violent earthquakes and volcanic eruptions; that from that time all communications between their people and the inhabitants of the "Lands of the West" had become interrupted; the occurrence having taken place 9,000 years before his visit to Egypt.

An account of that fearful event was also preserved by the learned men of Mayax who give of it a description identical with that given by the Egyptians. Nearly all the nations living on the western continent have kept the tradition of it, but they do not pretend that all mankind was destroyed.

In Mayax the learned priests caused a relation of it to be carved in intaglio on the stone that forms the lintel over the interior doorway in the rooms on the south side of their college. The building is known to this day by the name of *Akab-ɔib*, the dark, or terrible writing.

The author of the Troano MS., a work, I have already said, on geology, dedicates several pages at the beginning of the second part to the recital of that fearful cataclysm, and the phenomena which then took place. This leaves no longer room for doubting that a large continent existed in the middle of the Atlantic ocean, and which was destroyed within the memory of man; and that the narrative by Plato of the submersion of Atlantis is, in the main, correct. The Maya author represents the lost land by the figure of a black man with red lips, which would imply that it was mostly inhabited by a race of black men. In this case, the presence of black-skinned populations on the Western continent, anterior to the advent of the Spaniards, would be easily accounted for. The Mayas like the Egyptians, represented the world as an old man. Plutarch says they called East the face, North the right side, South the left side; this conception has reached our days, only we reckon the East as the right hand, West the left, North the face.

When the author of the Troano MS., speaks of the "Master of the land" par excellence, that is king Can deified, he pictures him sometimes with a human body, painted blue, and the head of a mastodon. On the façade of the building at Chichen Itza called by the natives *Kuna*, the house of God, to which Stephens, in his work on Yucatan, gives the name of *Iglesia*, is a tableau representing the worship of that great pachyderm, whose head, with its trunk, forms the principal ornament of the temples and palaces built by the members of king Can's family.

This tableau is composed of a face intended for that of the mastodon. Over the trunk and between the eyes formerly existed a human head, which has been destroyed by malignant hands. It wore a royal crown. This is still in place. On the front of it is a small portrait cut in the round of some very ancient personage. On each side of the head are square niches containing each two now headless statues, a male and a female; they are seated, not Indian fashion, squatting, but with the legs crossed and doubled under them, in a worshiping attitude. Each carries a symbol on their back; totem of the nation or tribe by which the mastodon was held sacred. Under these figures, are two triangles emblems of offerings and worship in Mayax as in Egypt. So also was the other symbol image of a honey-comb, an oblation most grateful to the gods, since with the bark of the Balche tree, honey formed the principal ingredient of *Balche*, that beverage so pleasing to their palate: the same that under the name of nectar, *Hebe* served to the inhabitants of Olympus. It is the *Amrita*, still enjoyed, on the day of the full moon, by the gods, the manes and the saints, according to the Hindoos; although it was the cause of the war between the gods and the Titans, and is the origin of many sanguinary quarrels among the tribes of equatorial Africa even in our days.

These symbols leave no doubt as to the fact that the personages represented by the statues are in the act of worshiping the mastodon.

The corona of the upper cornice, that above the mastodon's head, is formed of a peculiar wavy adornment often met with in the ornamentation of the monuments erected by the Cans. Emblematic of the serpent, it is composed of two letters N juxtaposed, monogram of Can . The corona of the lower cornice is made of two characters that read in Maya *Ah ɔam*, He of the throne—the monarch.

In Japan the seven members of the Can family, deified and figured by the same symbols as in Mayax, are worshiped today in the shrine of the palace at Tokio, dedicated to the goddess symbolized by a bird. This goddess calls to mind the goddess *Moo* of the Mayas, or Isis of the Egyptians. In the upper part of the shrine, over and above all the other attendants who have wings and beaked noses, is seen an elephant couchant, the god of fire standing on his back. In the midst of the flames that surround him is the head of a bird. So in Chichen we see the followers of queen Moo, who, we are informed by the author of the Troano MS. became the goddess of fire, carrying her totem, a bird, in their head-gears.

The Japanese claim to be offspring of the gods, and produce two different genealogical tables in support of their assertion. These gods amounting to *seven*, are said to have reigned an almost incalculable number of years in the country; although they assert that these primitive gods were spiritual substances, incorporeal. They were succeeded by *five* terrestrial spirits, or deified heroes, after whom appeared the Japanese themselves.

Here again we have a reminiscence, as it were, of the *twelve* gods, that the Egyptians told Herodotus, had governed their country, an incalculable number of years, before the reign of Menes their first terrestrial king. These gods were converted by the Greeks into the *twelve* deities, dwellers of the Olympus. The *twelve* serpent heads, brought to light by me in December, 1883, from the center of the mausoleum of the high-pontiff Cay, at Chichen-Itza, are emblematic of the *twelve* rulers, who had reigned in Mayax in times anterior to the great cataclysm when Atlantis was submerged; whose portraits, with the sign *cimi*, dead, adorn the east façade of the palace with the tableau of creation, showing that they existed in very early times. Of these rulers we again find a dim tradition in China in the *Tchi*, also called *che-cull-tse*—the *twelve* children of the emperor of Heaven, *Tien-Hoang*, who had the *body of a serpent*. Each of these *Tchi* are said to have lived eighteen thousand years, and to have reigned in times anterior to *Ti-hoang*, sovereign of the *country in the middle of the land*.

From this short digression let us return to the worship of the mastodon which we find very prevalent in India in that of the elephant *Ganesha*, the god of prudence, of wisdom, of letters, represented as a *red colored* man with the head of an elephant. He is invoked by the Hindoos of all sects at the outset of any business. No one would dream of writing a letter or a book without previously saluting Ganesha. His image is seen at the crossing of the roads, oftentimes decorated with a garland of flowers, the offering of some pious devotee. Architects place it in the foundation of every edifice. It is sculptured or painted at the door of every house as a protection against evil; at one of the entrances of every Hindoo city, that is called *Ganesha-pol*, as well as in some conspicuous door of the palace. We have already seen that in the most ancient edifices of Mayax the mastodon's head with its trunk is the principal and most common ornament. Are these mere coincidences? The name *Ganesha-pol* would be according to the Maya language, the *head of Ganesha*; *pol*, in Maya, being the head. If I wished to go further I might say that in *Ganesha* we have a dialectical pronounciation of *Can-ex*, "the serpents." No deity in the Hindoo pantheon is so often addressed; and his titles are so numerous that like Osiris it might be named *Myrionymus* "with ten thousand names."

So many are the legends accounting for the elephant head, it may be safely assumed that its origin is unknown. May not its worship have been introduced in India, with many other customs, that for instance of carrying the children astride on the hip; of printing an impression of the human hand, dipped in red liquid, on the walls of the temples and other sacred buildings by devotees etc.; by colonists from Mayax where these customs prevailed, and the worship of the mastodon was widely spread if not general? This surmise assumes the semblance of probability when we consider that the body of Ganesha is painted red, the color characteristic of the American race, and the symbol of nobility of race among the Egyptians.

The elephant was not among the animals worshiped by them. They do not seem to have been much acquainted with it. But the imprint of the red hand, so commonly seen on the walls of the temples of Mayax and India, has never been observed in the temples of Egypt; neither did the Egyptian women carry their children astride on their hip, as do still those of India and Yucatan, although many other customs were common to the people of these countries. It is probable that the colonists from the "Lands of the West" who settled in the valley of the Nile, replaced the worship of the mastodon, which did not exist in the country, by that of the bull, the largest and most useful of their domestic animals; and that this was the origin of their veneration for the bull Apis, as those who were initiated into the mysteries of Osiris well knew, being told that Apis ought to be regarded as a fair and beautiful image of their soul.

From the remotest antiquity the serpent was held by every people in the greatest veneration as the embodiment of divine wisdom. We have already said that Eusebius asserts that the Egyptians figured emblematically *Kneph*, the Creator, as a serpent; and that the Maya learned priests represented the engendered, the ancestor of all beings, in the sculptures, protected within the coils of the serpent. Mr. Stanyland Wake, in his book on the origin of the serpent worship writes: "the student of mythology knows that certain ideas were associated by the people of antiquity with the serpent, and that it was the favorite symbol of peculiar deities; but why that animal rather than any other was chosen for that purpose is yet uncertain."

The late Mr. James Fergusson in his work on "Serpent and Tree Worship," a work so full of erudition and interesting researches, whilst he conclusively shows that these worships were common to all civilized and half civilized nations of antiquity, fails to indicate the country where they originated. All authors who have written on the subject, admit that their origin is still an impenetrable mystery; although they agree that they are so intimately connected as to make it impossible not to believe it must have been the same.

The limited scope of this book does not allow me to give the matter all the space it deserves. I will therefore content myself, with bringing forth such facts as will conclusively show, at least to unprejudiced minds, that the serpent and tree worship indeed originated on this "Western continent," and from the same cause; "the love of the country," from the *amor-patriæ*, still so firmly rooted in the heart of the aborigines, that it is difficult to induce them to leave the spot where they are born, even to better their condition. Everywhere on the Eastern continents serpent worship is connected with mythological narratives, metaphysical speculations, or astronomical conceptions, far above the intellectual and scientific attainments of the mass of people among whom it prevailed.

These were mere fictions invented by the priests and learned men, to conceal either the real facts, or may be, their own ignorance of them. Still, anxious to maintain the preponderance and power that knowledge gave them over the multitudes, and having to satisfy their curiosity, they imagined such explanations as best suited the notions current in their times and the ideas of the people.

In early days the serpent, emblem of Kneph, the Creator, was the *agathodæmon*, the good genius. It is still so regarded by the Chinese, who consider it one of their most beautiful symbols. Later, when it became emblematical of *Set* or Typho, the slayer of Osiris, it was looked upon with horror, as the evil principle, the destroyer, the enemy of mankind. It has ever since continued to be so held by the Jews, the Christians, the Mahometans, in fact by all peoples whose religious tenets are founded on the Bible. If the tree and serpent were worshiped throughout the Eastern continents from the shores of the Atlantic ocean to those of the Pacific, from Scandinavia to Egypt and the Asiatic peninsulæ, their worship was not less spread amongst the nations that inhabited the "Lands of the West." We find vestiges of it everywhere on the Western continent; from the banks of Brush creek, in Adams county, in the State of Ohio, where still exists, on the crest of a mound, the effigy of a great serpent 700 feet long, entirely similar to that discovered by Mr. John S. Phené in Glen Feechan, Argyleshire, in Scotland, to the ancient city of Tiahuanuco, whose ruins are

13,500 feet above the level of the Pacific on the shores of lake Titicaca, near the frontier of Bolivia, on the high plateau of the Andes. There is yet to be seen a very remarkable doorway formed out of a single monolith 13 feet 5 inches long, 7 feet high above the ground, and 18 inches thick. This monolith has attracted the attention of d'Orbigny and the other travelers who, like myself, have been struck with astonishment by the beauty of the sculptures that adorn its south-eastern façade. Mayas, no doubt, were the unknown builders of that great city; since in the sculptures mentioned, we find, as in the temples of Japan, the totem of prince *Coh*, of his wife and sister *Moo*, and of their father king *CAN* (serpent).

I will make here a short digression in order to describe these sculptures, that with the knowledge we possess today of the history of the founders of the principal ruined cities of Mayax, afford us another proof that the builders of that city of Tiahuanuco belonged to a then highly civilized nation, which sent colonists to the remotest parts of the earth, as the English do today, and to whose historical annals may be traced many of the primitive traditions of mankind. This city was already in ruins when Manco Capac laid the foundation of the Inca's empire, and had been constructed by *giants before the sun shone in heaven*, as the natives said to the Spaniards when questioned as to its antiquity.

We have seen that the members of the family of king *Can*, are still worshiped in the temples of Japan, as of old they were in those of Egypt; we now meet unimpeachable records of them, carved on very ancient monuments, on the shores of lake Titicaca, at the foot of the great glaciers of Sorata and Illimani, as we have found them in mythological lore of India and Greece. Will it be said that these are mere coincidences?

The front of this monolithic gate was once upon a time as highly polished as the material, trachite, will permit. The whole space above the doorway is divided into four bands about eight inches high. The lower band contains seventeen small heads, in low relief, adorned in a somewhat similar manner to that of the central figure. *Seven* of these, those directly under that figure wear, like it, a badge that seems to be a plume composed of *three* feathers.

These small heads are separated by *grecques* having macaw's heads at their salient sides; these *grecques* are the symbol of power and strength. In the ancient Maya and Egyptian alphabets the *grecque* is equivalent to our latin letter H. *Ah* is the Maya masculine article, and it conveys to the mind the idea of might and power; this, taken in connection with the *macaw's* head, totem of Moo, the queen of Chichen, signifies the mighty, the powerful Moo.

The other bands are divided into squares of the same size, except in the center over the doorway, where there is a figure 32 by 21 inches.

Its head, the form of which is not only conventional, as its square eyes and mouth indicate, but likewise emblematical, consists of *three* superposed layers in the shape of escutcheons, the uppermost of which is sculptured so as to represent a human face. These *three* escutcheons as the *three* feathers of the plume that adorns it, the *triple* throne on which the figure seems to stand, the *three* dots on each cheek, the *three* oblong squares on the breast-plate, the *three* macaw's heads at the extremities of the *triple* sceptre it holds in its hands, are symbolical of the *three* great western regions that the Egyptians designated by the generic name of "*Lands of the West*" and represented by the character which is an image of the crown worn by some of the high chiefs in Mayax. That the central figure was meant to represent these countries, the sign, that stands in lieu of the mouth, indicates. It is the letter *M*, pronounced *Ma*, of the Maya and Egyptian ancient alphabets. It is the radical of *Mayax*, name of the Maya empire. But *Ma* in Egypt as in Mayax, is a word that signifies land, country, and by extension universe; and in Mayax as in Egypt is one of the signs for land.

The head is surrounded by rays divided into groups of four; four on the top, four on each side, and four on the under part. Each ray is terminated by a circle with a dot in the center, a sign very often met with on the monuments of Mayax; particularly on the trunk of the mastodon's heads. It is the first letter of the ancient Maya and Egyptian alphabets, and correspond to our letter A, the initial of the Maya word *Ahau*, king.

This would indicate that the central figure was likewise symbolical of the king *par excellence*, ruler of the empire, whom the kneeling personages that surround it, are in the act of worshiping as shown, not only by their posture, but also by the sign , carved on the neck of the macaw-headed figures, the followers of the queen *Moo* (macaw), which again in Mayax as in Egypt is the symbol of offering, worship, and adoration. The name of this great king we read in the four heads of leopards, terminating the rays at the upper angles, and those in the middle on each side of the escutcheon, and in the four rays of each group. Translating these symbols by means of the Maya language, we find that *Can Coh* was the name of the potentate; and that he was a member of the *Can* family, rulers of Mayax. This fact is indicated by the serpent heads at the lower angles of the escutcheon, those at the extremities of the breast-plate, the four oblong squares carved on the ribbons that support it, and the number of rays forming each group round the head.

In Maya *four* is *can*; but can also means *serpent*, likewise power. Number *four* according to Pythagoras, was particularly connected with Mercury, the *Thoth* of the Egyptians, as the deity who imparted intellectual gifts to man. The *Tetraktus* or number four represented the mystic name of the Creative Power; and in later times it meant *intellect, wisdom, all that is active.* Pythagoras asks: "How do you count?" Mercury: "one, two, three, four." Pythagoras: "Do you not see that what are four to you are ten and our oath? those (1, 2, 3, 4,) added together, forming ten, and four containing every number within it." The four leopard heads are his totem, *Kancoh, Coh* being leopard. Further on, I will refer more in detail to these personages, and to the rôle they have played in the civilization of the world, having been, and being still, worshiped in many countries under different names. The peculiar shape of the sceptre held in the left hand of the figure, the upper part of which is bifurcated, each end terminating with the head of a *macaw*, totem of the queen *Moo* of Chichen-Itza, sister and wife of *Coh*, and its undulations, like those of a serpent in motion, seem intended as an emblem of the three great regions that composed the empire that is likewise portrayed in the three rows of kneeling winged personages. The upper portion of said sceptre is symbolical of the Western continent, divided into two great parts united by the Isthmus of Panama. The lower was meant to represent that extensive island that sunk beneath the waves of the Atlantic ocean, about 11,500 years ago.

The sceptre held in the right hand of the central figure being whole, would show that the entire country was governed by a potentate to whom the rulers of the seventeen nations, into which the empire was divided, paid homage and acknowledged as their suzerain. These seventeen divisions of the empire are indicated by the seventeen small heads sculptured on the lower band, and the seventeen signs of land that adorned the arms, the breastplate, and the ribbon from which it is suspended.

Of the small kneeling winged figures, those of the middle row are portrayed with the heads of macaws to signify that they are the particular adherents of queen Moo, that here, as in Mayax, carry her totem as a badge or sign of recognition; whilst the others have human heads, but wear on their crowns her totem, in token that they recognize her as their *suzerain*. All these figures are ornamented with *twelve* serpents, arranged in groups of *three*, whilst the sash they carry across their body from the shoulder to the waist on the opposite side, terminates in a peculiar knot adorned with the four circles, that we have said stood for the word *Ahau*, that is king, indicating that their lord paramount is a member of the *Can* (serpent) dynasty. The whole tableau recalls vividly, that presented by the kneeling beaked nosed personages in attendance at the shrine of the bird deity at Kioto.

Mr. Angrand, the well known French archæologist, finds, and with reason, a coincidence between these sculptures and those of Central America, having a corresponding symbolical significance. In them he sees the proof of the identity of origin, of the intimate relationship of the builders of Tiahuanuco and those of Palenque, Ocosingo, and Xochicalco. He might have added, and be nearer to the truth, those of the cities of Mayax, that were founded many centuries before those mentioned by him.

In Mayax, it is where, indeed, the image of the serpent, as a symbol, is most commonly met with. We see it on almost every edifice in every city. It is one of the favorite ornaments, especially at Chichen-Itza, of which place it seems to have been the particular protecting genius. There it is found everywhere. It guards the entrance of all public edifices. It is at the foot of their grand stairways, as if defending the ascent. The columns that support their porticos are representations of it. Its head forms the base, its body the shaft. The nobles and other personages of high rank wore adornments made in the shape of serpents. Chichen may indeed be called the "*City of Serpents*" par excellence. If we, therefore, wish to know the true meaning of the serpent as a symbol, if we desire to inquire as to the motives that led to its worship, it is necessary to question the learned priests of that city; to consult the books in which the philosophers of Mayax have consigned their knowledge and their esoteric doctrines.

The origin of the "Serpent Worship" they tell us, can be traced to two apparently distinct causes. One, the esoteric, taught only to a few select of those initiated in the greater mysteries, is the homage to be tributed by the creature to the Creator. The other, the exoteric, inculcated on the uninitiated, was the love of the country, and the respect due by the subjects to their rulers, living images and vicars of the Deity on earth.

In order to comprehend the first, or esoteric, we must recall to mind that Eusebius says that the Egyptians represented emblematically *Kneph* the Creator, and the world also, under the figure of a serpent, which, Horapollo asserts, was of a blue color with yellow scales; but they fail to inform us as to what may have been their motives for thus symbolizing the First Cause; or from whom they had received this symbol, that was the same used by the Mayas. A clue to this mystery can no doubt be found in the cosmogonical notions prevalent among the ancient civilized nations; for, strange to say, they seem to have been alike with all. We read in the *Manava-dharma-sastra* that the visible universe in the beginning was nothing but darkness. Then the great, self-existing Power dispelled that darkness, and appeared in all His splendor. He first produced the waters; and on them moved *Narayana* the divine spirit.

Berosus, recounting the ancient legend of the creation according to the Chaldeans, says: "In the beginning all was darkness and water; and therein were generated monstrous animals and strange and peculiar forms.... A woman ruleth them all." Her name in Chaldee is *Thalath*, in Greek *Thalassa* (the sea), that is in Maya *Thallac* (a thing without steadiness).

Genesis recounts that: "In the beginning the Earth was without form and void; and darkness was upon the face of the deep, and the spirit of God moved upon the face of the water. And God said, Let there be light and there was light."

In *Primander*, that modern critics consider the most ancient and authentic of the first philosophical books of Egypt, attributed to Hermes Trismegistus, in the dialogue between *Thoth* and Primander, the Supreme Intelligence, we read these words of *Thoth*. "I had then before my eyes a most prodigious spectacle. All things had resolved themselves into light. A marvellous, pleasing and seducing sight it was to contemplate. It filled me with delight. After a while a horrid shadow, which ended in oblique folds, and assumed a humid nature, agitated itself with terrific noise. From it escaped smoke with uproar, and a voice was heard above the din. It seemed as the voice of the light; and the verb came forth from that voice of light; that verb was carried upon the humid principle. Out of it came forth the fire pure and light, and rising, it was lost in the air that, spirit-like, occupies the intermediate space between the water and the fire. The earth and the water were so mixed that the surface of the Earth covered by the water appeared nowhere."

And in what are termed the modern Hermetic books, the origin of things is thus explained: "The principle of all things existing is God, and the intellect, and nature, and matter, and energy, and fate, and *conclusion*, and *renovation*. For there were boundless darkness in the abyss, and water, and a subtle spirit, intellectual in power, existing in chaos. But the holy light broke forth, and the elements were produced from among the sand of a watery essence."

In the *Popol-Vuh*, the sacred book of the Quiches, we read: "This is the recital of how everything was without life, calm and silent, all was motionless and quiet; void was the immensity of the heavens; the face of the Earth did not manifest itself yet; only the tranquil sea was, and the space of the heavens. All was immobility and silence in the darkness, in the night; only the Creator, the Maker, the Dominator, the Serpent covered with feathers, they who engender, they who create, were on the waters as an ever increasing light. They are surrounded by green and blue, their name is Gucumatz."

We have already said how the Maya sages have taken care to perpetuate their cosmogonical conceptions, by causing the narrative of the creation to be carved, in high relief, over the doorway of the east façade of the palace at Chichen-Itza, and that these conceptions were identical with those of the Hindoos and the Egyptians. It cannot be argued that this identity of ideas about the origin of things, arrived at by the wise men of India, Egypt, and Mayax, and expressed in as nearly the same words as the genius of the vernacular of these various countries admits, is purely accidental; or, that they have arrived separately at the same conclusions on the subject, without communicating one with the other. The notion and its explanation must have originated with one, and been taught to the others just as our modern scientific discoveries, or religious beliefs, are carried from country to country, even the most remote, and made known to their inhabitants. What should we think of the man who would pretend that the railway, electric telegraph, and many other of the latest inventions, instead of having originated in one particular country, nay, more, in the brain of a particular man, have sprung simultaneously among all the various nations which make use of them? Would not that man be regarded as a born idiot or a fit subject for a lunatic asylum? We can easily understand how these cosmogonical notions have passed from the Egyptians to the Chaldees or to the Hindoos or *vice versa*; but who brought them to the "Lands of the West" and when? Who can say they did not arise among the inhabitants of the "Western continent;" and were not conveyed by them to the other nations?

In my work "The Monuments of Mayax," I have shown how the legends accompanying the images of several of the Egyptian deities, when interpreted by means of the Maya language, point directly to Mayax as the birthplace of the Egyptian civilization. How the ancient Maya hieratic alphabet, discovered by me, is as near alike to the ancient hieratic alphabet of the Egyptians as two alphabets can possibly be, forcing upon us the conclusion that the Mayas and the Egyptians either learned the art of writing from the same masters, or that the Egyptians learned it from the Mayas. There is every reason to believe that the cosmogonical conceptions, so widely spread, originated with the Mayas, and were communicated by them to all the other nations among which we find their name.

An analysis of the tableau of creation, carved on the façade of the palace at Chichen-Itza, cannot fail, therefore, to prove interesting. In it we shall find a proof of the scientific attainments of its designers; and also the reason why the serpent came to be worshiped all over the Earth.

The philosophers of Mayax must have known that the waters cover the greatest part of the globe (about three fifths); and that water being a combination of gases (oxygen and hydrogen), the most subtle of fluids, must have been the first form of matter produced. This is why on each side and on the top of the tableau they placed the symbol of water ; taking care to leave without it, at the upper part, a portion equal to two-fifths of its length. In the midst of the waters they represented the figure of an egg, that is a germ. Why an egg and not any other seed? Is it because their study of physiology had made them acquainted with the fact, that no being exists on Earth, but that is born from an egg? They represented the egg emitting rays. The rays of the light into which says Thoth, all things resolved themselves; that, says the Quiche, author of the Popol-Vuh, appeared on the water as an increasing brightness that bathed the Creator, the *feathered serpent*, the *Kneph*, as the Egyptians would name it, in green and azure. It is well to notice that the symbols of water terminate with the head of serpents; because they compared the waves of the ocean to the undulations of the serpent's body while in motion.

For this reason the Mayas named the sea *Canah*, the great, the powerful serpent: and in the Troano MS., the sea is always designated by a serpent's head. This explains why the Quiches, the Mayas, the Egyptians, the Hindoos, represented the world, and, by extension, the maker of it, as a serpent. Thus it is that they placed a serpent within the egg, behind the creator to indicate that this symbol is the totem of the ancestor of all beings. And here we have one of the origins of the serpent worship: that is, the adoration of the Creator.

In Egypt the goddess *Uati*, the genius of the lower country, is at times represented as a serpent with inflated breast, the body standing erect over a basket or sieve, the lower part resting against a figure resembling our numeral. At times again, as a winged serpent, with inflated breast, wearing on its head a cap or crown of peculiar shape, that it is said to be the crown of lower Egypt. Why the Egyptians selected such symbols to represent the lower country, we are not informed; and it is doubtful if the learned Egyptologists could explain the motive.

Now it is a most remarkable fact, that these are the very symbols used by the Maya hierogrammatists and artists to figure their own motherland, the Maya empire.

The author of the Troano MS., sometimes pictures Mayax as a serpent with an inflated breast (Plate. XVII., Part II.), at other times as a serpent with part of the body bent in the shape of the Yucatan peninsula, and the artists who executed the paintings in the funereal chamber of Prince *Coh*, typified the country as a winged serpent, with the back painted green, the belly yellow, wearing a blue crown on the head, its tail ending with a peculiar dart resembling in general contour the southern continent of America.

This is not the place to give minute explanations of these symbols which I have considered in another work, I simply wish to consign here such facts as cannot be attributed altogether to hazard. So the peculiar twist against which rests the body of the serpent, emblem of the lower country, is exactly the same that forms the symbol used in the Troano MS., to represent the gulf of Mexico and the Caribbean sea, whose waters bathe the peninsula of Yucatan, that seems as if standing erect between them as the serpent in the Egyptian sign.

As to the sieve, it is called, by the natives of that country, *MAYAB*. Mayab was, in past ages, one of the names of the peninsula. The crown of Lower Egypt , is precisely that worn by certain chieftains, whose portraits we see in the bas-reliefs at Chichen-Itza. There the peak was worn in front; in Egypt at the back: may be as a mark of respect on the part of the Egyptians toward their mother country, to signify that as the child, Egypt must stand behind its parent, as it is customary for children to do among the aborigines of Yucatan.

Since the Egyptians and the Mayas used identical signs as symbols of the country in which they lived, may it not be inferred that the same cause prompted their selection? We must not lose sight of the fact that the winged serpents introduced into the paintings of Egypt, are merely emblematic representations connected with the mysterious rites of the dead, and the mode of being in Amenti; that is, in the "Lands of the West" where the souls of the departed were supposed to return and exist, after being liberated from their mortal body.

In early days *Uati* or *Mati*, the country of Mayax, was one of the divinities, worshiped by the settlers on the banks of the Nile; and the asp, not any other snake, played a conspicuous part in the religious mysteries, and was universally honored.

Here, again, we may ask why? What possible relation can exist between the asp and the country; between the asp and the office of king or the attributes of Deity? Still it was the badge of royalty, worn as an ornament on the head-dress of kings and gods. Is the selection of the asp as a mark of distinction to be ascribed to a mere whim? May not that predilection be assigned to the fact that, when angry, it dilates its breast; and when in that condition it recalled to the minds of the colonists, the geographical contours of the land of their forefathers in the West, and the way it was represented in the books, from which they had studied in their childhood? If we look at a map of the Western continent, it will be easy to perceive that the contours of Central America—that is the Maya empire of old—figure a serpent with an inflated breast, in a position similar to that of the emblem of lower Egypt, the head being the peninsula of Yucatan, anciently the seat of the government; and that the southern continent would be the dart of its tail, as pictured by the Maya artists. The green color of its back, the verdant, tropical forests that cover the land; the yellow belly, the internal volcanic fires, that cause the surface to wriggle like a serpent; the blue crown on its head, the blue canopy of heaven above; the wings, the smoke of the volcanoes; the fins, the high peaks of the chain of mountains that traverses the country from north to south, part of the Cordilleras, that are as the backbone of the continent.

The intense love of their country is one of the most striking characteristics of the aborigines to the present day. That love may be said to amount to fanaticism. In it we find another origin of the serpent worship, emblem of the motherland.

In the Serpent mantra, in the *Aytareya Brahmana*, a passage speaks of the Earth as the *Sarpa Rajni*, the queen of the serpents, and the mother of all that moves, still worshiped by the Nayas, dwellers in the valley of Cashmere.

In Mayax the primitive rulers derived their title *CAN* (serpent) from the shape of the contours of their empire, as the priests of the sun received theirs from the name *Kin* of that luminary. Their emblem however, was not a winged serpent, with a dart at the end of the tail, but a rattlesnake covered with feathers; image of the feathered mantle used by the king, the high-pontiff, and other high dignitaries, as ceremonial dress. This feathered rattlesnake adorns the walls of the royal mansions. It is seen at Uxmal, on the east façade of the west wing of king *Can's* palace and at other places. After their death these rulers, images of Deity on earth, received the honors of apotheosis. They became gods and goddesses and were worshiped as such. In Assyria the symbol of the winged serpent was replaced by that of the winged circle, emblem of Asshur, the supreme deity of the Assyrians; and this symbol is seldom found in the sculptures except in immediate connection with the monarch. It seems to be also closely related with the sacred or symbolical tree.

Here again, is another origin of "Serpent Worship," in that of the kings of Mayax under the symbol of the "feathered serpent." One of the names for rattlesnake, in Maya, is *Ahau-Can*, the royal serpent. In the sculptures the king is often represented by this emblem with *seven* rattles at the end of the tail; seven having been the number of the members of king *Can's* family. In Egypt the kings and queens were honored as gods after their death. In Greece and other countries, the heroes were deified and worshiped as divinities.

From all antiquity and by all nations, the tree and serpent worship have been so closely identified, as to guarantee the inference that their origin is the same, although it seems difficult to comprehend what possible analogy may exist between them, without a knowledge of the place where they originated, of the people that first instituted it, of their traditions and peculiar notions. Many learned students have published the results of their researches on the subject. None, however, has yet assigned a birthplace to the tree or serpent worship.

The late Mr. James Fergusson tells us that he is inclined to believe that it was in "the mud of the lower Euphrates, among a people of Turanian origin, and spread thence to every country of the old world." This is truly indefinite. Then comes the query: what about the tree and serpent worship among the inhabitants of the Western continent? For they also had their sacred trees; and with them as with the natives of the Eastern world, the tree was symbolical of eternal life.

The oak tree was dedicated to *Baal*, the chief god of the Phœnicians and other eastern nations. Under it the Druids performed their most sacred rites in honor of *Œseus*, the Supreme Being. The ash was venerated by the

Scandinavians. The inhabitants of the island of Delos believe the gigantic palm tree to be the favorite production of Latona. The people of Samos, Athens, Dodona, Arcadia, worshiped in sacred groves, as those of Canaan. In India the worship of the tree is of very ancient date, as in the island of Ceylon: in the courtyard of every monastery a bo-tree (ficus Indicus) is planted. Nowhere, however, do we find the origin of that worship mentioned.

Mr. Fergusson advises us to look to the Egyptians, these being the most ancient civilized people, for an explanation of it, averring that it undoubtedly prevailed among them before the multifarious Theban pantheon was elaborated. In Egypt the tamarisk was the holy tree chosen to overshadow the supposed sepulchre of Osiris, the king of Amenti. The *persea* was sacred to Athor, the regent of the West, often identified with Isis. The sycamore was consecrated to Nut, mother of Isis and Osiris, frequently represented in the paintings of the tombs, standing in its branches, pouring from a vase, a liquid which the soul of the departed, under the form of a bird with a human head, catches in his hands. It is the water of eternal life. So the trees were particularly sacred to the deities connected with Amenti, that is, to the deified kings and queens from the "Lands of the West."

We are told that the sacred tree was an emblem found in frequent association with the "winged circle" in Assyria. As this symbol is always met with in immediate connection with the monarchs, it would seem that the worship of the tree bears a close relation to, if it is not typical of, that of the deified heroes and kings.

To understand the relationship between the tree, the winged serpent or "circle" and the "monarchs" it is again necessary to consult the annals left carved in stone or written in their books by the wise men of Mayax. From them we learn that the Mayas held certain trees sacred, Landa, Cogolludo, and other early writers tell us that, even as far down as the time of the Spanish conquest, the aborigines believed in the immortality of the soul, that would be rewarded or punished in the life beyond the grave, for its deeds whilst in the body.

Their reward was to consist in dwelling in a delectable place, where pain was unknown, where there would be an abundance of delicious food, which they would enjoy, with eternal repose, in the cool shade beneath the evergreen and spreading branches of the *yaxché* (ceiba tree), which is found planted, even today, in front of the main entrance of the churches, throughout Yucatan and Central America. Sometimes the churches are built in the midst of groves of ceiba trees, that in some localities are replaced by the gigantic palm tree (*Palma real*).

The Maya empire was of old, according to the author of the Troano MS., figured as a tree, planted in the continent known today as South America, its principal branch being formed by the Yucatecan peninsula. Here we have the key to the origin of the tree worship, and its intimate relation to the winged serpent and the king. It is again the worship of the country symbolized by a tree, as it also was by a serpent, or by the Ruler. Thus we find a natural explanation of the tradition current among the ancient nations, that the TREE *par excellence*, the tree of life, that is of civilization, of knowledge, was placed in the middle of the land, of the garden, of the primitive country (*Mayax*) of the race; the empire of the Mayas being placed between the two great continents, North and South America, forming the "Lands of the West."

This relation of the tree, the serpent and the country in the middle of the World, is confirmed by the Chinese writers, commentators on the *Chou-king*, one of the most ancient literary monuments of China. Speaking of the Tien-Hoang or kings of heaven, Yong-chi says: *Tien-hoang had the body of a serpent. He was the origin of letters. He gave names to the ten KAN, and to the twelve Tchi, in order to determine the place of the year*; and *Yuen-leao-fan*, another writer, says that KAN *means the trunk of a tree, and that* TCHI *are the branches, reason why they are called* CHE-CULL-TSE, *the twelve children*. It is well to remark here that the children of king *Can* were called CAN-CHI, which is still a family name among the aborigines.

TI-HUANG, king of the Earth, is also called *Hoang-kiun*, that is, he who reigns sovereignly in the middle of the earth, and also *TSE-YUEN*, or the son principle, the engendered, the *Brahma* of the Hindoos, the *Kneph* of the Egyptians, the *Mehen* of the Mayas.

The cross is another sacred symbol much reverenced by all nations, civilized and semi-civilized, ages before the establishment of Christianity: and although we find representations of it in almost every part of the world, from its mere delineation scratched on the rock, to the stately temples and admirably hewn caves of Elephanta in India, still nowhere do we learn of its origin. There are several varieties of crosses, but all may be traced back to the primitive form which resembles the Latin cross.

Among the earliest type known on the Eastern continents is the "Cruz Ansata," called the "Key of the Nile." It was the "symbol of symbols" among the Egyptians, the Phœnicians and the Chaldees, being the emblem of the *life to come*. It was placed on the breast of the deceased, sometimes as a simple on the fulcrum *of a cone*; sometimes represented as supported on a heart. It is also seen adorning the breasts of statues and statuettes in Palenque, Copan, and other ancient cities of Guatemala, Nicaragua, and various localities of Central America. Everywhere it was associated with *water*. In Babylon it was the emblem of *water deities*. In Egypt, Assyria, and Britain, it was emblematical of *creative power and eternity*. In India, China, and Scandinavia of *heaven and immortality*. In Mayax of *rejuvenescence and freedom from physical suffering*. The cross, as a symbol, was placed on the breast of the initiate after his new birth was accomplished in the Bacchic and Eleusinian mysteries.

Remesal and Torquemada assert, in their respective works, that when in 1519, the Spaniards, under Hernan Cortez, landed at the island of Cozumel, they found crosses which the natives worshiped as gods in their temples. After them many writers, on their authority, have affirmed the same thing. This, however, seems to have been a mistake. Bernal Diaz del Castillo, who accompanied Cortez, does not mention the existence of such symbols in Cozumel, but emphatically says that Cortez, having ordered the destruction of the idols that were in the sanctuaries, caused an image of the Virgin Mary to be placed in their stead, and near it a wooden cross, made by two of his carpenters, to be erected, recommending the natives to take great care of them when he left. Dr. Pedro Sanchez de Aguilar, another of the early writers, maintains that the stone crosses found afterward in the island were made in imitation of that of Cortez; and Bishop Landa, although a most zealous missionary, intent on converting the aborigines to the Catholic faith, does not mention the existence of crosses in Cozumel before the advent of the Spaniards; a fact he would certainly have taken advantage of in his predication of the gospel, and would not have failed to mention in his work, had he been satisfied that the symbol really existed.

There can be no doubt that in Mayax, in very remote ages, the cross was an emblem pertaining to the sacred mysteries. No external vestiges of the symbol are to be found among the remains of the temples and palaces of the Mayas, such as those seen at Palenque and other places of Central America. Only one image of a perfect cross have I ever met with in the ancient edifices of Yucatan besides the ground plan of the sanctuary at Uxmal. It forms part of the inscription carved on the lintel of the doorway of the east façade of the palace at Chichen. Still tradition tells us that the cross was symbolical of the "*God of Rain*." If so, they made no image of it, nor did they celebrate any festival in honor of it at the time of the conquest, but held it simply as a notion of their forefathers.

The ancient Maya astronomers had observed that at a certain period of the year, at the beginning of our month of May, that owes its name to the goddess MAYA, *the good dame, mother of the gods*, the "*Southern Cross*," appears perfectly perpendicular above the line of the southern horizon. This is why the Catholic church celebrates the feast of the *exaltation of the holy cross* on the third day of that month, which it has consecrated particularly to the *Mother of God*, the *Good Lady*, the virgin *Ma-R-ia*, or the goddess Isis anthropomorphised by Bishop Cyril of Alexandria.

In all localities situated within the 12th and 23d degree of latitude north, about the beginning of January, the dry season sets in and no more rain falls during several months. In May and April in the countries like Yucatan, where there is no water on the surface of the ground, all things become parched; the trees and shrubs lose their leaves, nature looks desolate, all living beings thirst for a drop of moisture, the birds and other wild creatures, mad with thirst, lose their characteristic shyness and venture near the haunts of man, imperiling their lives in search of water; death, for want of it, seems to threaten all creation.

But four bright stars appear in the south. A shining cross stands erect above the southern horizon. It is the heavenly messenger that brings good tidings to all, for it announces that the flood-gates of heaven soon shall be open; that the so longed for rain will shortly descend from on high, and with it joy and happiness, new life to all creatures. Man hails with thankful heart, welcomes with songs of gladness, this brilliant harbinger of the *life to come*, for indeed it is a god for him, the GOD OF RAIN that *rejuvenates nature, frees man and all other creatures from physical sufferings, brings felicity to them—heaven therefore—*and, with renewed life, *immortality*. Is it not the creative power that is eternally renovating and revivifying all things on the surface of the earth? Is it then strange that all nations, in every age, should have worshiped the cross as symbol of the *life to come* and *immortality*, and held it in so great veneration? It must be remembered that all the civilized nations in the "Lands of the West" and in the "Eastern Continent," dwelt in latitudes where the constellation known as "the Southern Cross" is visible during the month of May, and that the first showers soon follow its apparition above the horizon. From these of course it was transmitted to the others further north, that accepted the symbol, without understanding its meaning, and in aftertimes many speculations have been indulged in concerning its origin: but the unsophisticated natives, in the midst of their forests today, rejoice at the sight of the "Southern Cross" and prepare to sow their fields.

The origin and meaning of the mystical , that symbol of "hidden wisdom" as it has been denominated by scholars of our days, found on all Egyptian monuments, in the temples, in the hands of the gods, in the tombs on the breast of the mummies, also met with in the ancient edifices of Mayax, and on the statues and altars in the temples at Palenque, has given rise to many speculations on the part of modern savants. They have not reached yet any conclusion, although its name TAU says plainly, that it is nothing more or less than a representation of the "*God of Rain*" the "Southern Cross." Effectively *tau* is a Maya word composed of the three primitives *ti*, here, *a* for *ha,* water, and *u* month, which translated freely means "*This is the month for water*;" hence for the resurrection of nature—for the new life to come.

The complex form of the mystical which is formed of a cone with two arms extending, one each side, and an oval placed immediately above them, has been denominated by the Egyptologists *cruz-ansata*. It is not of Egyptian origin. It has its prototype in the conoidal pillar, surmounted by a sphere, used by the Babylonians as symbol of life and death; death being but the beginning or nursery of life. This emblem was only a reminiscence of the *yaxche*, the sacred tree of the Mayas, under the roots of which, the natives assert, is always to be found a source of pure cold water. The trunk of the yaxche, from the foot to the top, forms a perfect cone from which the main branches shoot in an horizontal direction. Its leafy top, seen from a distance, presents the appearance of a half sphere of verdure. The *cone*, the *tau* and the *cruz-ansata* were for those initiated to the mysteries the same symbol, emblematical of Deity, of the life to come, of the dual powers, of fertility. The Mayas and other peoples of Central America, in the sculptures or paintings, always represented their sacred trees with two branches shooting horizontally from the top of the trunk, thus presenting the appearance of a cross or tau.

In straying apparently so far from the main object of these pages, and tracing to their true origin the primitive traditions of mankind and many of the religious symbols common to all the civilized nations of antiquity, by dispelling the mists that have accumulated around them in the long vista of ages, my aim has been to show that they all emanated from one and the same source, and that this source was the country of Mayax, in the "Lands of the West." Ancient sacred mysteries, have been celebrated in the temples of Egypt, Chaldea, and India, from ages so remote that it is no longer known by whom or where they were first instituted. Herodotus tells us that the daughters of Danaus instituted the Thesmophoria in honor of the goddess Ceres, in imitation of the mysteries celebrated in Egypt in honor of Isis, and taught them to the Pelasgic women. That Eumolpus, king of Eleusis, instituted in his own country the Eleusinian mysteries on his return from Egypt, where he had been initiated by the priests as Orpheus who founded in Thracia those that bear his name; but who taught the rites of initiation, the use of the symbols and their meaning, to the Hierophants of Egypt, to the magi of Chaldea, to the Gymnosophists of India?

The mode of initiation, the use of the same symbols, with an identical signification ascribed to them, by peoples living so far apart whose customs and manners were so unlike, whose religion, so far at least as external practices were concerned, differed so widely, show that these mysteries originated with one people, and were carried to and promulgated among the others. As we do not find it mentioned anywhere that they originated either with the Egyptians, Chaldees, or Hindoos, and we have seen that their primitive traditions have been derived from the history of the early rulers of Mayax, is it not natural that we should look for the institution of the mysteries among the Mayas, since we find the same mysterious symbols, used by the initiates in all the other countries, carved on the walls of the temples of their gods, and the palaces of their kings? Their history may afford the clue to the original meaning of said symbols, as their language has given us the true signification of the words used by the celebrating priest to dismiss the initiates in the Eleusinian mysteries, or by the Brahmins at the end of their religious ceremonies, and as it has revealed the so long hidden mystery of the mystical *TAU*.

That sacred mysteries were celebrated from times immemorial in the temples of Mayax, Xibalba, Nachan (Palenque of today), Copan and other places of Central America there can be no doubt, since besides the symbols sculptured on the walls of the temples and palaces, in two distinct instances, we see the rites and the trials of initiation described in the Popol-Vuh; and as these rites and trials were identical with those to which the applicants to initiation in the mysteries of Egypt, Greece, Chaldea and India were subjected, we are justified in seeking in Mayax for the causes that may have induced the founders of the sacred mysteries to select the odd numbers 3, 5, and 7, instead of the even 2, 4, and 6 for mystic numbers.

The symbolization of number 3 may possibly be accounted for in two different ways. One is suggested by the sceptre of Poseidon, that Plato says was the first king of Atlantis, and is represented by the Greek mythologists as being a son of Kronos; his three-pronged trident being an allusion to the *three* great islands that formed his kingdom, North and South America and Atlan, that now lies buried under the waves of the Atlantic ocean. The emblem placed in the hands of *Vul* the god of the atmosphere in the Chaldean mythology, found also in those of the Hindoo gods, may likewise represent the three worlds or great regions that the Egyptian and Maya hierogrammatists designed by the character in the hieroglyph for the name of the "Lands of the West," which the latter also figured as the sacred tree with three branches, a simile of which we find in Scandinavia, in the *three roots* of the sacred ash Yggdrasil, mystic-world tree, and the *three* heavens, and the three worlds whose destruction, by water, was prophesied by Vishnu.

The deification of the "World" composed of three parts forming a great whole, may have been the origin of the Trimourti, or Triune god, so prevalent among the ancient nations of antiquity, and probably led to the mystification of number 3. We find it symbolized all over the earth, in every nation. We see it in Mayax in the three platforms on which are raised the most ancient edifices; in the three rooms that formed the temple where the mysteries were performed; in the three steps that led to the first or lower platform in all sacred edifices; in the 21 metres (3×7) of all the principal pyramids in Yucatan; in the three concentric circles of the Zodiac. We meet with it constantly in India, in the *vyahritis* or three sacred words; the three ornaments or *saranas*; the three principal classes; the three ways of salvation; the three fetters of the soul or *gunas*; the three eyes in Siva's forehead; the three strands of the sacred cord worn by the initiates of the three principal classes; the three letters of the sacred word A.u.m. In Egypt the three thonged flagelum of Osiris; the triple phallus carried in procession at the festival of the Paamylia in honor of the birth of Osiris, and also the triads, as likewise in Chaldea.

Another way of accounting for the mystification of number 3, is by taking heed of the indications of Orpheus, Plato, Proclus, and the other Greek philosophers who had been admitted to the participation of the secrets communicated in the mysteries to those worthy of being entrusted with them. They tell us that the *three* intellects of the Demiurgos, of the triple deity, were "*three kings*."

The author of the Troano MS., relates at some length the history of the three sons of king *Can*; and of the troubles that arose among them when, after the death of their father, the reins of the government fell into their hands. Of that fact a faint tradition, very much distorted, seems to have still existed among the aborigines of Central America at the time of the Spanish conquest; for Bishop Landa states: "That it was said that once upon a time three lords, brothers, governed the country together." Those three brothers, sons of king *Can*, are realities, personages who have certainly lived a mundane existence, since we not only have their portraits, their weapons, and their ornaments, but also their mortal remains. They recall vividly the three sons of Adam, the three sons of Seb, and the three sons of Kronos. The author of the Troano MS., informs us that the members of the family of king *Can* were deified after their death, and worshiped in temples, the ruins of which still exist buried in the depths of the forests of Yucatan under a shroud of verdure. It is not at all improbable that *Cay*, the elder brother and high-pontiff having instituted with his father the sacred mysteries, took as symbol of the various degrees into which they divided them, the number of the members of their family, in order to perpetuate their name and history through the coming ages. This explanation seems the more plausible, if we remember that Eusebius tells us that the Egyptians represented the supreme Deity under the shape of a serpent (Canhel) that was as superior to the triads, as the father is to his children in whom he rejoices. "*Numero Deus impare gaudet*." In this connection the *three Hoang-ti*, of Chinese mythological times, might also be mentioned. They too had the shape of serpents.

Among the ancient civilized nations of the eastern continents number 5 was also considered mystic. Frequent mention is made of it in their sacred books. In China it occupies a conspicuous place among the celestial or perfect numbers, as 1, 3, 5, 7, 9, are called in the *y-king*, or Canonical book of Changes; a very ancient work, so highly esteemed by the wise philosopher Confucius (Kong-fou-tse) that he was seldom seen without it. There we read of the five elements, water, fire, wood, metal, and earth; of the five kinds of grain; of the five colors, black, red, green or blue, yellow and white; of the five tastes, salt, bitter, sour, acid, and sweet; of the five tones in music; of the five relations of life between men; those between a king and its ministers, a father and his children, a husband and his wife, elder and younger brothers, and between friends; of the five virtues, philanthropy, uprightness, decorum, prudence, fidelity; of the five organs of the body, kidneys, heart, liver, lungs, and spleen; of the five Chang-ti, or elementary generations; of the five parts that form the heavens; of the five seasons of the year; of the five genii that govern the five elements; of the five principal mountains of the empire; of the five tutelary mountains.

In India number 5 is also very prevalent in things pertaining particularly to psychological conceptions or religious observances; so they speak of the five organs of intelligence, by means of which the external objects are perceived; of the five organs of action; the five elements, the five great oblations; of the five great sacrifices; the five great fires, etc. In Mayax it was likewise a mystic number, since we find this simbol carved at each end of the southern apartment in the edifice consecrated to the celebration of the sacred mysteries. It appears in the number of steps leading from the courtyards or terraces to the principal apartments in the "House of the Governor," "the palace of king *Can*" and other edifices at Uxmal, and in other buildings. It is the number particularly set apart for the second of the three platforms that compose the base on which all the ancient temples and palaces of the Mayas are raised. In the rites of modern Freemasonry, it is still the sacred number related to the second degree. In the Troano MS., the legends of all the compartments into which the work is divided, as in chapters, are composed of five characters, to indicate that said legends are the headings, that is *ho-ol*, the beginning, the head.

This number may have become sacred, in the mysteries, among the Mayas, in remembrance of the number of the children of king *Can*; for besides his three sons *Cay*, *Aac*, and *Coh*, he had, by his wife *Zoo*, two daughters, *Moo* and *Nicte*, whose names bear a striking resemblance to *T-Mau*, one of the names of Isis and *Nike* her sister. So king *Can* by his wife *Zoɔ*, had five children, just as *Seb* had by his wife *Nut* in Egypt; these being *Aroeris*, *Set*, *Osiris*, *Isis*, and *Nike*. Strange coincidence, that may, however, give us a knowledge of the origin of the mystification of number five.

SEVEN seems to have been the sacred number *par excellence* among all civilized nations of antiquity. Why? This query has never been satisfactorily answered. Each separate people has given a different explanation, according to the peculiar tenets of their religion. That it was the number of numbers for those initiated to the sacred mysteries there can be no doubt. Pythagoras, who had borrowed his ideas on numbers from the Egyptians, calls it the "Vehicle of life," containing body and soul, since it is formed of a quartenary, that is: *Wisdom and Intellect*; and a *trinity* or *action* and *matter*. Emperor Julian, in *Matrem* and in *Oratio*, expresses himself thus: "Were I to touch upon the initiation into our secret mysteries, which the Chaldees bacchised, respecting the *seven-rayed* god, lighting up the soul through him, I should say things unknown to the rabble, very unknown, but well known to the blessed Theurgists."

Whatever that knowledge may have been, and their esoteric explanation of the cause of the mystification of number seven, can only be surmised today; but it is not improbable that it was to be found in some event in the early history of the race whose traditions we find scattered broadcast over the Earth. We have seen that the family of king *Can* was composed of *seven members*, who became rulers of the *seven* cities that bear their names, the ruins of which still exist in the forests of Yucatan, and by the beauty and richness of the ornamentation, the massiveness and finish of the walls of their temples and palaces, excite the admiration of the beholder. These personages, deified after their death, have been worshiped in various countries, and are yet in some, under different names. May not the remembrance of the existence of these *seven* ancient rulers of Mayax, have been the origin of the tradition of the *seven* divine rulers of Egypt; of the *seven Manous* that according to the Brahmins, governed the world in the night of times; of the *seven Richis* or holy personages who assisted them; of the *seven princes* of the Persian court; and the *seven councillors* of the king; of the *seven Ameshaspants* or first angels; of the *seven great gods* of the Assyrians; or the *seven primitive gods* regarded by the Japanese as their ancestors and said by them to have governed the world during an incalculable number of years; of the *seven Cabiri*, worshiped by the Pelasgians at Lemnos and Samothracia; the *seven* great gods in theogony of the Nahuatls? Do we not see a simile of the *Ah Ac chapat* or *seven-headed* serpent of the Mayas, totem of their *seven primitive Rulers*, that is of the *seven members* of king *Can's* family, in the *seven-headed heavenly Serpent* on which rests Vishnu, the Indian creator, that corresponds to the Egyptian *Kneph* or the *Mehen* (*Canhel*) of the Mayas; or in the *seven* serpents that form the crown of *Siva*; or again in the *Seven-rayed god Heptaktis*, of which the emperor Julian was so reluctant to speak?

It would seem that the duration of certain religious festivals was fixed to commemorate the existence on Earth of these *seven* primitive gods or rulers, the tradition of which we find in all countries where we meet with vestiges of the Mayas. So we see the *seven days* of the festival of the Eleusinian mysteries; the *seven days* of the festival in honor of the bull Apis, a symbol of Osiris; the *seven days* of the feast of the tabernacles. The septenary system was also adopted for the same purpose no doubt, in Mayax, since we find the *seven* cities dedicated to each of the members of king Can's family; the *seven* pyramids that adorned the city of Uxmal; the *seven* turrets that ornamented the south façade of the north wing of king Can's palace at Uxmal, each turret inscribed with the name of one of the members of his family; those dedicated to the females being on the east end of the wing. The *seven gradients* into which is divided the third or uppermost of the three platforms that serve as a substructure to the temples and palaces; the *seven superposed gradients*, forming all the pyramids calling to mind the *seven terraces* of the temple of the *seven* lights at Borsippa, the most perfect form of Chaldee "temple tower," and the "pyramid degrees" at Sakkara, although in this Egyptian pyramid the gradients are more numerous. The *seven rooms* built on the west side of the conical mound that supports the temple in which the mysteries were performed at Uxmal: each room again being dedicated to one of the members of king Can's family; the bust of the person to whom it was consecrated being affixed over the doorway. The *seven courses* of the stones used in the construction of the walls and of the triangular arches that form the ceilings of the rooms. The same system prevails in the arrangement of the grand gallery in the centre of the great pyramid at Ghizzeh in Egypt. In that monument as in all the antique edifices of Mayax, the proportional scale followed by the architects in the drawing of their plans is in accordance with the numbers 3, 5, 7, and their multiples.

The predilection of the nations of antiquity in which the sacred mysteries were celebrated, for number *seven* appears in many ways. The *seven days* that the rainfall that produced the deluge lasted, according to the Chaldeans, is reproduced in the *seven days* of the prophesy of the deluge by Vishnu to Satyravata, as we read of it in the *Bhagavata purana*; and the *seven days* of the prophesy of the same event, made by the Lord to Noah, according to Genesis; on account of the *seven days* of rainfall the Babylonian priests used *seven vases* in the sacrifices; and in the hierarchy of Mazdeism, the *seven Marouts* or genii of the winds; the *seven rounds* of the ladder in the cave of Mithra. The Aryans had the *seven horses* that drew the chariot of the sun; the *seven Apris* or shapes of the flame; the *seven rays of Agni*; the *seven steps* of Buddha at his birth. The Egyptians had divided their nation into *seven classes*; the week into *seven days*: according to them the creation was completed in *seven days*. Among the Hebrews, we find the *seven lamps* of the ark, and of Zacharias vision; the *seven branches* of the golden candlestick; the *seven days* of the feast of the dedication of the temple; the *seven years of plenty; and the seven years of famine*. In the Christian dispensation, the *seven churches* with the *seven angels* at their head; the *seven golden candlesticks*; the *seven heads* of the beast that rose from the sea; the *seven seals* of the book; the *seven trumpets* of the angels; the *seven vials* full of the wrath of God; the *seven last plagues* of Apocalypse. In Greek mythology, the *seven heads* of the hydra killed by Hercules, the *seven islands* sacred to Proserpine mentioned by Proclus.

The prevalence of *seven* as a mystic number among the inhabitants of the "Western Continent" is not less remarkable. It frequently occurs in the *Popol-Vuh*. We find it besides in the *seven families* said by Sahagun and Clavigero to have accompanied the mystical personage named *Votan*, the reputed founder of the great city of Nachan, identified by some with Palenque. In the *seven caves* from which the ancestors of the Nahualts are reported to have emerged. In the *seven cities* of Cibola, described by Coronado and Niza, the site of which has been accurately fixed by Mr. Frank Cushing in the immediate neighborhood of the village of Zuñi. In the *seven Antilles*; in the *Seven heroes* who, we are told, escaped the deluge.

Can it be maintained that this acceptation of *seven* as a mystic number by nations so heterogeneous and living so far apart, and from the remotest ages, is purely accidental? The origin of its mystification has never been explained. It has been transmitted to us by our predecessors, who themselves had accepted it from theirs, without knowing why it was made the sacred number of the third degree in the rites of initiation into Freemasonry. True, in receiving the degree the initiated are told the esoteric meaning attached to it in modern times; but this meaning does not give the origin of its mystification. In fact, it is an invention of our days.

That it was the sacred number of the highest degree of the sacred mysteries in Mayax is evident. We have seen that 3 was the number of the male children of king Can; 5 that of his sons and daughters; 7 was consequently that of the members of the whole family. It is not therefore improbable that to commemorate that fact, 7 was made the sacred number of the third degree of their sacred mysteries, and that this was the origin of its mystification.

In these pages I have presented, without commentaries, a few of the facts that twelve years researches among the ruins of the antique temples and palaces of the Mayas, a knowledge of their language (still spoken by their descendants, and in some places, as in the vicinity of Peten, in all its pristine purity); the deciphering of certain mural inscriptions; the study of the sacred book of the Quiches, and the interpretation of passages in the

Troano MS., have disclosed to me concerning the history, civilization, cosmogonical conceptions, religious tenets and practices of the ancient inhabitants of Yucatan.

It is for you, reader, to judge if such facts are worth your consideration, and of the truthfulness of my assertion that a knowledge of the history of the primitive dwellers in these "Lands of the West" will help to raise the veil that has covered during so many centuries the origin of the first traditions of mankind. Although in the first annual report of the executive committee of the "Archæological institute of America," we read that: "The study of American archæology relates indeed to the monuments of a race that never attained to a high degree of civilization and that has left no trustworthy records of continuous history. It was a race whose intelligence was for the most part of a low order, whose sentiments and emotions were confined within a narrow range, and whose imagination was never quickened to find expression of itself in poetic or artistic forms of beauty. From what it was or what it did, nothing is to be learned that has any direct bearing on the progress of civilization." With all due respect for the learning of the gentlemen who have attached their names to so astounding an assertion, I beg to differ from their opinion expressed so emphatically. I differ because I have seen and photographed the constructions left by the mighty races that have preceded us on this continent. They have not. Because I have studied for years, *in situ*, these monuments that attest to the high civilization of their builders. They have not. Because I have learned the language in which they have consigned part at least of their history in inscriptions carved on stones, and read some of said inscriptions. They have not. Indeed, on this continent, not far from New Orleans, exist the relics of past generations which are as interesting, if not more so, as those of Egypt, Babylonia, Greece, and Italy; as deserving the attention of all students of archæology, of history, of ethnology, and philology. It is time yet to save from utter destruction the last records of ancient American history, that are crumbling every day more and more, and are being destroyed by the hand of ignorance and cupidity. A few years more, and all intelligible traces of them will have disappeared. Will nothing be done in this country to preserve what remains of the ancient American civilization? Of that civilization which seems to have been the fountain-head at which the philosophers of all nations, in the remotest antiquity, have come to acquire knowledge and drink inspiration from the learning and wisdom of the Maya sages.

Americans have established in Athens schools for the study of Greek Archæology; in Alexandria, for the decipherment of the inscriptions carved on the walls of the temples, on the obelisks, and in the papyri found in the tombs in Egypt; is it not time that students in United States should direct their attention to the ancient history of the continent on which they live? It is not altogether lost, and the tongue in which it is written is not a dead language. Maya is one of the oldest forms of speech, cöeval, if not anterior to Sanscrit. The names Alpha, Beta, Gamma, etc., etc., of the letters of the Greek alphabet, form a curious epic poem in that language. There are many interesting inscriptions in it that only await decipherment to illumine the past records of the race in America. Many of these precious documents exist in the City of New York. They will reveal the history of the mighty nations that have dwelt on this "Western Continent;" they will tell us of the origin of many of our primitive traditions. Why then not found in Yucatan, in the midst of the ruins of the temples and colleges of the learned priesthood of Mayax, a school where students of American archæology can learn with their language, what the Maya sages knew of man's origin, of his intellectual development, of the past of their people, of the colonists they sent to other parts of the world, where they carried the arts, sciences, and religion of the mother country and its civilization from which our own is descended?

After twelve years of incessant labors and great hardships, unaided by any government or scientific society, having to encounter opposition, and surmount countless difficulties placed maliciously in our way by those whose duty it should have been to afford us all protection, robbed of our finds by the Mexican government which has even refused to indemnify us for the money expended in making these discoveries, Mrs. Le Plongeon and myself, after saving from destruction many important documents and relics, have at last found a key that will unlock the door of that chamber of mysteries. Shall it be allowed to remain closed much longer? We have lifted, in part at least, the veil that has hung so long over the history of mankind in America in remote ages. Shall it be allowed to fall again? Will no efforts be made by American students, by men of wealth and leisure in the United States, to remove it altogether?

www.ingramcontent.com/pod-product-compliance
Lightning Source LLC
Chambersburg PA
CBHW040510110526
44587CB00045B/4214